THE THINKING PERSON'S
BIG BATHROOM BOOK OF ETERNAL
QUOTES AND OBSCURE ONE-LINERS
FROM THE BEGINNING
TO THE PRESENT
TO THE END

THE THINKING PERSON'S BIG BATHROOM BOOK OF ETERNAL QUOTES AND OBSCURE ONE-LINERS FROM THE BEGINNING TO THE PRESENT TO THE END

BY HAROLD M. ELLIOTT

FIRST EDITION

First Printing: 2018

ISBN-13: 978-1986829571

ISBN-10: 198682957X

A 001
Before the beginning, there
was Bupkis .... *Yhwh*
Before the beginning, there
was the Logos...............................*Plato*
Before the beginning, there
was the Dao............................ *Lao tze*
Before the beginning, there
was Om .... *Ancient Hindu Rishis*
Before the beginning was
Asha.......................................*Zoroaster*

A 002
Plato's Logos (aka, the Word) lives on
in Christianity as the spiritus sancti (the
invisible ghost)........... *Philo of Alexandria*
The Logos was not in the Hebrew
texts, so it was kept out of the
Vulgate .... *Jerome of Illyria*

A 003
Before the beginning, there was
nothing except formless
chaos.......................................*Xu Zheng*
Before the beginning, everything was
calm, silent, motionless, and the sky
was empty ....*Mayan Popol Vuh*
Before the beginning, there was no
earth and no sky...............*Mother Nature*
Before the beginning, there
was darkness and
formless chaos...................*The Wu Wang*
Before the beginning, there also
was Yin, Yang, and Qi..............*Zhou Yan*

A 004
In the beginning, there was a
primordial atom or singularity of
infinite density........................... *Lemaitre*
In the beginning, there
was the Big Bang ....*Hoyle*
Cosmology begins with the
Big Bang...................................... *Koberlein*
After the Big Bang, the Earth was
formed and is now over
4.5 billion years old........................*USGS*

A 005
Speculation about what existed before
The Big Bang or what stars and
galaxies are moving into or
through has yielded little
or nothing ....*Hawking 1942–2018*

A 006
When God began to create heaven
and earth, the earth was unformed
and void, with darkness over
the surface of
the deep ....*The Tanakh*
In the beginning, God created Heaven
and the Earth, which was without form
and void, and darkness was upon the
face of the deep, and God said "Let
there be light.".........*The King James Bible*

A 007
In the beginning, God made the
heavens and the earth out of nothing,
and the earth was idle and void, and
the darkness was on the face of the
deep................... *The John Wycliffe Bible*

A 008
In the beginning, God created heaven
and earth, and the earth was void
and empty, and the dark was
upon the deep, and the spirit
of God moved upon the
waters .... *The John Tyndale Bible*

A 009
Praise God and pass the
ammunition.......... *The John Wayne Bible*
Read this Deistic version of
the four canonical
Gospels....... *The Thomas Jefferson Bible*
Let there be
Lite Beer............*The Adolph Coors Bible*

A 010
In the beginning, there was nothing
except Ahura Mazda, living in the
Endless Light, and Ahriman (the evil
spirit) living in absolute darkness.
Between the two was
complete emptiness ...... *The Bundahishm*
Then Ahura Mazda created the sky,
the earth, fire, life, the first
man, Gayomard, and a subordinate
deity, Mithras ....*Zoroaster*

A 011
In the beginning were the ways of
nature, existing before heaven
and earth, silent,
and void.....................*The Tao Te Ching*
Then chaos coalesced into a cosmic
egg where the forces of yin and yang
existed in perfect balance...Then Pan-
gu emerged from the cosmic egg and
began to create the earth and the
universe...........................*The Wu Wang*
After many years of creation, Pan-gu
became tired and he/she departed
and left the world intact and
harmonious.............................*Xu Zheng*

A 012
In the beginning were the self-created
and all-powerful sun gods, Amun-Ra
and Ptah. And Ptah created
the world.........................*Pyramid Texts*
Also, in the beginning were the gods
Anu, Enlil (El), Enki, Ba'al, Ishtar,
Elohim, and Marduk ......*Mesopotamian &*
Canaanite priests
All laws are now written
in stone......................*Sargon I of Akkad*

A 013a
In the beginning, there was neither
existence nor non-existence.
All was chaos, void
and formless ....*The Mahabharata*

A 013b
In the beginning, Lord Brahma
made the Earth out
of nothing .... *Vedic scriptures*
In the beginning was the ultimate
reality that was Brahman, with whom
was the word Om, and the word
was Brahman....................*The Yajurveda*

A 014
In the beginning there was God, the
Demiurge, and his Archons
(messengers). Then the Demiurge
created the material world and
everything in it ....*Early Gnostic writings*

A 015
In the beginning, there was absolute
good and absolute evil, with nothing
in between ....*The Prophet Mani*

A 016
The life works of the great Phoenician
historian Sanchuniathon records the
history of Phoenicia and Byblos (that
some say is the world's
oldest city) ....*Philo of Byblos*
The great Vizier of Egypt,
Imhotep, built the
first pyramid.............. *The Pharaoh Djoser*
I translated the
hieroglyphics.......................*Champollion*
The ancient ruins of Harappa and
Mohenjodaro of the Indus Valley
Civilization are still mysteries, and their
script remains undecipherable......... *John*
Marshall

A 017
After the beginning was Buga and
the primordial sea ...... *Tungusic shamans*
Long ago, all was mixed up
together in darkness.................*The Kojiki*
After the beginning, there were
demons and gods who churned up
the seas and made the
elixir of life ....*Lord Vishnu*

A 018
Mt. Fuji and bears are sacred to all
Ainus in Japan. Ainus used to live all
over Honshu, but now they only live in
Hokkaido and northern Honshu. After
the beginning, Izanagi and Izanami
stirred up the primeval ocean and
made the Islands of Nippon. Then
they begat Amaterasu, the Sun
Goddess, from whom all Japanese
emperors descend .... *The Nihon Shoki*

A 019
After the beginning, there was Gaia
(Jee-ah), the life-giving
Mother Earth .... *Greek Orogeny*
After the beginning, Chronos made
Aether and Chaos ..... *Hesiod's Theogony*

A 020
After the beginning was the divine
blacksmith......................... *William Blake*
These giant stone alignments can
predict seasons and
eclipses .... *Officiants of Stonehenge*
This great Irish burial mound
also marks winter
solstices............. *Officiants of Newgrange*
We've forgotten the purpose of
these stone alignments in
Armorica .... *Officiants of Carnac*
Nobody knows why and who the
people were who built the recently
discovered, large, multiple structures at
the Gobekli Tepe archaeology site near
the border between
Turkey and Syria .... *Klaus Schmidt*

B 001a
Before the beginning were the gods
In-Dagda & Dis Pater
(Father Dis)......... *Irish druids or shamans*
After the beginning, there was the god
Djous Pater............. *Proto-Italic shamans*

B 001b
After the beginning, there was the god
Dyaus Pitr............... *Sanskritic Brahmans*
After the beginning, there was the
high god Zeus................ *Greek hierarchs*
After the beginning were Odin, Ash,
Elm, and Ziu (Tiw)..... *Germanic shamans*
After the beginning was the high god
Ius Pater.............. *Early Roman sacerdos*
After the beginning was the high
god Jupiter........... *Later Roman sacerdos*
After the beginning, there was
the sacred tree
Yggdrasil .... *The Teutonic Eddas*
After the beginning was
the sacred fire, Atar .... *Zoroastrian
priests*

B 002
Long ago, there were many ways of
divining the future, and there were
ancient Chinese fortune-tellers who
recorded them in a book called the
Book of Changes, also known as
the I-Ching (I-Jing), which is false and
totally worthless .... *Confucius*

B 003
Long ago, Chinese naturalists sought
harmony with nature and found ways of
reading landscapes, wind, and water,
so as to correctly orient houses,
graves, roads, buildings, rooms,
beds, and tombs .... *Ancient feng shui
masters*

B 004
For centuries, ancient martial arts
experts in China developed many
different ways of self-defense, such as
kung-fu, tai-chi, kung-pao, judo,
mai-tai, falun-gong, la-shi,
wushu, and dofu .... *Chop Chop*
I was Hollywood's blackest belt
kung-fu, karate, and
karaoke master .... *Bruce Lee*

B 005
After the beginning, God created man
and woman out of dust, sand, and clay
in his/her own image ....*The Torah*
After the beginning, Allah created man
out of a clot of blood (Alaq)............ *Koran*
Then God made
little people ....*Book of Gnomes*

B 006
There were giants in those
early days ....*Books of Genesis
& Numbers*
These giants, called Nephrolites, were
the sons of Abanaki, and were believed
to be Anarchists (messengers)
from God....................... *Book of Eunoch*

B 007
After the creation, God created a
primeval marsh garden with four rivers
flowing into and through it............*Book of
Genesis*
Would you like a
pineapple? ....*Eve*
Yeah, original sin my ass,
gimme one....................................*Adam*
Can I have one too?..... *The Montypython*

B 008
All Egyptians must now worship
only the new god, Aton.............. *Ikhnaton*
That didn't work out very well.......*Nefertiti*
Didn't work out for
me either...........................*Tutankhamen*

B 009
In ancient Egypt, there were many
high priests of Amun-Ra in
Upper and Lower Egypt
(Kemet)....................*The Pyramid Texts*
Deceased Egyptian notables must be
embalmed and buried in tombs
from which they would arise and
pass through many tests before
entering the Field of
Reeds (Aratu)........ *The Book of the Dead*

B 010
Let those people go.....................*Ramses*
Watch my people go ....*Moses*
Watch me part the Red Sea ....*Heston*
Watch these walls come down......*Joshua*
I could have done that
all by myself.............................. *Samson*
Keep moving, wife, and don't
look back toward where the
sodomites are ....*Lot*

B 011
I am what I am ....*Burning bush*
I yam what I yam.........................*Popeye*
I am the great I am........... *Prince Charles*
I do not like this spam ....*Steve Jobs*
I do not like green eggs & ham ....*Dr.
Seuss*

B 012
Are there any righteous men?....*Abraham*
Are there any honest men? ......*Diogenes*
Are there any good men?......*Tom Cruise*
Are there any clean men? ....*Mr. Clean*
Are there any sober men?............*Alanon*
Are there any happy men? ....*Pinterest*
Are there any Mets who
can play this game? ....*Stengel*

B 013
First, do no harm....................*Hippocrates*
To do or not to do?.......................*Omelet*
To do is to be............................... *Sartre*
To be is to do....................................*Kant*
Skoobie doobie do ....*Sinatra*

B 014a
I am one of the keepers of the Chinvat
Bridge. All Zardushts and Parsis who
have good thoughts and good deeds
can cross over the bridge into
paradise ....*Mithras*
Those who have evil thoughts and
deeds will fall off the bridge into the
fiery abyss below ....*Zoroaster*

B 014h
In Islam, unbelievers will fall into
the bottomless pit
down under.................. *The Grand Muffin*
All Jihadistas go to paradise
without passing Go......... *Mohamet al sod*

C 001
All Jewish dead will enter and remain
in Sheol, a dark place in the shadowy
underworld. After death, all Jews will
go to Sheol regardless of whether they
were righteous or wicked during life.
Some Orthodox Jews claim to have
an afterlife................... *Talmudic scholars*

C 002
In Mexico, many people commune with
their departed loved ones on the Dios
de la Muerte.................. *Ancient customs*
among Aztecs, Zapotecs,
Mixtecs, & Mayans

C 003
We are angels and recorders of deeds
of those Muslims who wish to cross
over the Bridge of Sarrat into paradise
(Jannah). The unrighteous will
fall off into the bad places
below (Jahanna).............. *Munkar & Nakir*

C 004
Not know life? How can
one know death?..................... *Kungfuzi*

C 005a
The Hsiung-nu barbarians have
always ravaged northern
China............................ *Ssu-ma Ch'ien*

C 005b
I am the first emperor, and all history
begins with me............. *Qin Shi Huang Di*
I completed much of the Great Wall
to keep the northern Xunu barbarians
out of China............. *Ch'in Shih Huang Ti*
I completed much of the Grand Canal,
which greatly improved travel from the
south to the north of China ....*Sui Yang Di*

C 006
During the Ming dynasty, I sailed out
with my fleet of sea-going junks from
China to the South Seas, India,
Arabia, and Africa, and then
returned......................................*Admiral*
Zheng He
I never sailed from China to any
of the Americas.........................*Hui Shen*

C 007
I sent a brave naval invasion force
against Nippon, but the Chinese
junks were poorly built and
a typhoon sank all of them
and the attack failed....... *The Great Khan*
The Mongol naval attack on Nippon
was blown away by a great typhoon,
which will always be known in Japan
as the divine wind
(Kamikaze) .... *The Emperor Go-Uda*

C 008
First know your place in
society..................................... *Kungfuzi*
Then seek harmony in
society............................. ......*Confucius*
Practice ethical behavior in
society..................................... *Mencius*
Seek and practice universal
love ....*Mo Di*
All men are selfish and need harsh
laws to keep themselves from
bad conduct........................... *Han Feizi*

C 009
Teach a man to fish, and he may eat
nothing but fish forever .... *Hillel*
Seek harmony in nature, and practice
simplicity, patience, and
compassion................................... *Laozi*
Learning to say "I don't know" is the
first step to true wisdom............... *Moses
Maimonides*

C 010
Practice peace and
nonviolence............................... *Gandhi*
Eat no meat, grow no crops, and
practice absolute Ahimsa.......... *Mahavira*
Eat no beans........................ *Pythagoras*
Practice peace and nonviolence
to all living creatures................ *Siddharta
Gautama*
Build retirement pastures for aged
and infirm work animals...... *Asoka's Pillar
Edicts*

C 011
Years ago, in Xanadu, a stately
pleasure palace
I did decree.......................... *Kublai Khan*
How many Mongols does it take
to make a horde? .... *Genghis Wong*
Try my Mongol kosher BBQ........ *Genghis
Cohen*
Many man smoke, but .... *Fu Manchu*
I'm lost.................................... *Wong Wei*
I'm in hiding................................. *Lei Lo*

C 012
On the road to
Shangri-la .... *Hope & Crosby*
The ever-ever man in never-never land
sends his greetings .... *The High Lama*
Tibet isn't really part
of China....................... *The Dalai Lama*
I am not a fake lama........ *Panchen Lama*
Just me and my llama....... *Sesame Street*
My llama is numero uno........ *Bruno of the
Pampas*

D 001
We keep the prayer wheels
spinning........................... *Tibetan Monks*
I will be taking Buddhism over
the mountains into China.... *Bodhidharma*
I will come later .... *Avalokiteshvara
(Guanyin)*

D 002
Seek virtue and proper
behavior in society .... *Master Kung*
Seek freedom from passion,
joy, and grief................................. *Zeno*
Seek tranquility and modest
pleasures................................. *Epicurus*
When there's no life, there's no
hope................................... *Cicero*

D 003
We possess all things .... *Qian Long*
The emperor was not impressed
with our gifts .... *Lord McCartney*
Burn all the opium .... *Commissioner Lin
Zexu*

D 004
I am the younger brother of Jesus
Christ and the soldiers of my Taiping
tien-guo will drive all foreign Devils out
of China........................... *Hong Xiuquan*
My army will defend Shanghai against
the Taipings................ *General "Chinese"
Gordon*
Nanjing has now been taken from the
Taiping revolutionaries .... *Zeng Guofan*

D 005
China must adopt new programs
of self-strengthening...... *Chang Chih-tung*
Chinese backwardness must end,
and we must adopt western systems
of technology .... *Li Hung-chang*
Help us take back Peking from
the Boxers .... *Dowager Empress Cixi*
We must cut off our queues and get rid
of the hated Manchus...................... *Sun
Chung-shan*

D 006
I did not betray the revolution, and stop
calling me "bullet-head" .... *Yuan Shih-k'ai*
Peking will now be known as
Beiping, and stop calling me
the "peanut" .... *Chiang Kai-shek*
Why should railroads have
such bad feng shui? ....*Sun Yat-sen*
One belt, one railroad..............*Xi Jinping*

D 007
Throughout history, China has had
many communistic regimes (including
mine) and has had many land
reforms .... *Wang Mang*
When the enemy tires, advance.....*Sun Zi*
Power comes from the
barrel of a gun.................... *Mao Zedong*

D 008
Hide your strength and
bide your time .... *Deng Xiaoping*
How do you get all
those girls? .... *Zhou Enlai*
Power is the ultimate
aphrodisiac .... *Kissinger*

E 001
I was the last emperor ....*Henry Puyi*
Me too ....*Romulus*
So was I.................................*Napoleon*
I was also............................*Montezuma*
Moi aussi ....*Louis XVI*
Ja ich auch .... *Wilhelm II*

E 002a
One must spend a long time with
mouth open waiting for roast
duck to fly in.............................*Won Ton*
There's been a terrible car accident
outside. Anyone want some
newly pressed Peking
duck?.............................*Chiang kai-chef*

E 002b
Egg rolls with your
roast beast?............................*Hop-Sing*
Chop Suey or Chow Mein with
your Tsing Tao?................ *Charlie Chow*
No, we now use pinyin, so bring me a
nice Qing Dao instead,
xie hsieh...................................... *Don Ho*

E 003
Fry me to the Moon................... *Ali Wong*
Just me and my basketball .... *Yao Ming*
Just me and my yoyo .... *Yo-yo Ma*
They call me the Dog Meat General,
but it's a board game, not
something to eat .... *Gen. Zhang*

E 004
Yanks Battle Reds .... *1950 news
headlines*
We are defending the Puson
Perimeter......... *General "Bulldog" Walker*
We will land at
Inchon ....*Douglas MacArthur*
We're headed north to the Yalu .... *MAC*
You're relieved................................*HST*
We'll settle for the 38th parallel.......... *IKE*

E 005
Would you like dog or cat with
your kimchi? .... *Humjob Park*
I hit more home runs than
anyone else...................... *Sadaharu Oh*
Someday, Seoul will be the
capital of all Korea. .... *Syngman Rhee*
I am not crazy .... *Kim Jong un-hinged*

E 006
I was the best king of Siam for a
short time ....*Yul B.
Chulalongkorn*
We are Siamese if you please, or even
if you don't please .... *Siamese twin cats*

E 007
Come see my new liquor and wine
store in Los Angeles........*Nguyen Cao Ky*
No spitting on my
sidewalks........................ *Lee Kuan Yew*
Qing Ganbei........................*General Tso*
Who dat don dar?..................... *Cao Dai*

F 001
Long ago, we explored the Black Sea,
but we never found any golden fleece,
just a few sheep skins lying on the
bottom of a river........................ *Jason &*
the Argonauts

F 002
We defeated the Trojans by giving
them a fake horse .... *Agamemnon*
Wooden walls will
not fail............................. *Delphic Oracle*
We've won at Marathon and Salamis…
pant, pant, pant................... *Pheidippides*

F 003
Where did those two go? ....*King Minos*
Watch me fly high.......................... *Icarus*
Don't fly too close to the sun..... *Daedelus*
All is fire and instability .... *Heraclitus*
Now you have fire .... *Prometheus*
Keep the bonfires burning...... *Zarathustra*
Thus spake Zarathustra........... *Nietzsche*

F 004
All is water and change .... *Thales*
The water goes round and around,
and it comes out here.......... *Archimedes*
Water, water, everywhere and
not a drop to drink .... *Coleridge*
Once upon a time, a Phoenician
ocean-going fleet circumnavigated all
of Africa in three years............*Herodotus*

F 005a
All are atoms...................... *Democritus*
All is quantification .... *Pythagoras*
All is geometry .... *Euclid*
All is storytelling .... *Homer*

F 005b
All is sophistry.......................*Protagoras*
All is on the map ....*Strabo*
All is geo-musicology ....*Alan Lomax*
All is geography .... *Claudius Ptolemy*
All is in my library...............*Eratosthenes*

F 006
All is questioning....................... *Socrates*
All is justice.............................. *Justinian*
All is law ....*Lycurgus*
All is reform .... *Solon*
All is war.. *Mars*
All is strength .... *Hercules*
All is fluting ....*Pan*
All is cleansing............................... *Ajax*
All is vanity ....*Narcissus*

F 007
In vino veritas ....*Pliny the Elder*
Vino, vedi, vici.............................*Caesar*
Vino, viagra, valium...................... *Hefner*
Vino pluribus............................*Dionysus*
Vino, vino, vino ....*Bacchus*
Vino, alter ego, libido.....................*Freud*
Vino, vino, toga ....*Belushi*
Vino into aqua converti........*Wrong Jesus*
In vino beatus ....*Ben Franklin*
Vino bonum lasts into eternity........*Cicero*
Vino, vino, vitae ....*Beringer Bros.*
Vino, olive oil, vendetta ...... *Vito Corleone*
Vino, vintage, superbus.............*Mondavi*
Vino is no more....................... *Eliot Ness*

F 008
All is drama..............................*Euripides*
All is sleep ....*Morpheus*
All is wandering.......................*Odysseus*
All is golden ....*Midas*
All is illusion..................................*Plato*
All is matter................................ *Aristotle*
All is fertility .... *Cybal*
All is moderation ....*Euripides*
All is gluttony ....*Trimalchio*
All is overindulgence ....*Henry VIII*
All is battle.................................*Leonidas*

F 009

All is defending the bridge............ *Horatio*
All is mine ....*Cyrus*
All is more.....................................*Xerxes*
All is now mine ....*Alexander*
All was mine.................................*Darius*
All is tragedy ....*Sophocles*
All is biography.........................*Plutarch*
All are eggs.................................. *Ovid*
All is oratory.................................*Cicero*

F 010

All is erotica .... *Onan*
All are projections.....................*Mercator*
All is duty ....*Cincinnatus*
All is living well ....*Seneca*
Living well is the best revenge .... *Geo.*
Herbert

F 011

Anno urbis conditae...................*Romulus*
Ab urbe condita........................ *Titus Livy*
In omnibus Aeneid .... *Virgil*
Delenda est Romae.....................*Tarquin*
The western seas
are ours .... *Carthaginians*
Delenda est Carthago..................... *Cato*
Delenda Romae est...................*Hannibal*
In Hoc Signo Vinces............ *Constantine*

F 012

SPQR (Senatus
Populusqe Romanus)............*Senate and People of Rome*
The die is cast, and we will cross the
Rubicon in the morning.......*Julius Caesar*
Sic transit gloria
(all glory is fleeting) ....*Slave whispering into Caesar's ear*
Caesar is dead.............. *Marcus Antonius*
All roads now lead to Rome .... *Octavian*

F 013

Why should I not
sack Rome?......................*Attila the Hun*
Because it isn't nice ....*Pope Leo I*
Read my book on Attila the Hun's
management techniques .....*Wes Roberts*
I did not fiddle while
Rome burned................................. *Nero*
We put down the
Jewish revolt..........................*Vespasian*
The empire is now too large and
must be split up into pieces ......*Diocletian*

F 014

All roads now lead to
nowhere .... *Alaric the Visigoth*
We defeated Attila and his allies at
Chalons......... *Theodoric & Flavius Aetius*
Some Huns fled east through
Switzerland and some settled
there................................. *Francis Lieber*

G 001

Corpus delicti.................. *Agatha Christie*
Magna Carta............... *King John the Bad*
Magnum opus............. *Will & Ariel Durant*
Magna carpa................... *Beached whale*
Magna banyo...............*El Chapo Guzman*
Maximum flatus............... *Wind in his hair*
Status quo .... *Warren G. Harding*
Caveat emptor ....*Charles Ponzi*
Mea culpa................................*Yoko Ono*
Nihil sine ration ....*Leibniz*
Quid pro quo.........................*Luca Brazzi*
Modus operandi............. *Sergeant Friday*
Excreto ergo sum..................... *Descartes*
Esse est percipi .... *George Berkeley*

G 002

All is triangular .... *Pascal*
All is statistical ....*Gauss*
All is existential .... *Kierkegaard*
All is dancing ....*Zorba*
All is living long .... *Methuselah*
All is staying young ....*Peter Pan*

G 003

All is new clothes..................... *Emperor*
All is no clothes................... *Bettie Paige*
All is vulgarity....................... *Redd Foxx*
All is fortune telling .... *Madam Zenobia*
All is forgery............................*Mister 880*
All is relative............................ *Einstein*
All is gravity.............................. *Newton*
All is genius............................ *Amadeus*
All is mediocrity .... *Solieri*
All is misogyny .... *Menken*

G 004

All men are born depraved and
damned .... *Augustine*
All unbaptized infants are
damned .... *Calvin*
All men are born good
and free .... *Pelagius*
All men are intrinsically good ......*Petrarch*
All men are born evil
and unfree .... *John Knox*
All men are condemned to
be free... *Sartre*

G 005

In nomine patris, et filii, et spiritus
sancti....................................... *Pontifex*
Maximus
In nomine patris, et filii, et spiritus
scampi............................. *Chef Marisco*
de Mazatlán
In nomine pasta, et filii, et spiritus
chianti........................... *Tuscan vintners*
In nomine patris, et filii, et non-kosher
pizza............................. *Chef Goyardee*
In nomine pastry, et filii, et spiritus
spaghetti........................... *Chef Bocuse*
In nomine patris, et filii, et
spiritus tiki...................... *Thor Heyerdahl*
In nomine lobos, et lupus, et spiritus
canine...........................*Dances with*
werewolves

G 006

All men have free will .... *Augustine*
All men are created equal............... *John*
Hancock
All men are created unequal.....*George III*
All men are born unequal ....*Jeff Davis*
All men are equal before fish........*Hoover*
All fish rot from the head down ....*Dukakis*

G 007

O'Sama sleeps with the fishes.... *O'Bama*
So it has been written............*Mohammed*
(PB&J)
I am the emperor of the sea........*Neptune*
Raindrops keep falling
on my head........................... *Goeff Love*
It rained for 40 days
and 40 nights.................................*Noah*
Row, row, row, your boat........ *Gilgamesh*
I'm just singing in the rain....... *Gene Kelly*

G 008

I am the ruler of the ocean.........*Poseidon*
I am the Prince of Whales ....*Moby Dick*
One of our orcas ate one of our
trainers, so we are now freeing all our
dolphins and orcas so they can swim
happily and freely in all the world's
oceans .... *Utah Marine Fish-World Circus*
Free Willy .... *John Wayne Bobbitt*

G 009

I sailed down the coast of western
Africa and then returned
because it was getting
too hot..................... *Henry the Navigator*
I sailed south around southern Africa
and then went on to India............. *Vasco*
da Gama
I will call it the Pacific Ocean ....*Balboa*
I was the first to sail around the
world ....*Magellan*
I discovered
California.................... *Sir Francis Drake*

G 010
Stop calling me the chicken of the
sea ....*Capt. Franco Schettino*
Britannia rules the waves........ *William IV*
Stop killing baby fur seals ....*Angry
Canadians*

G 011
When Adam delved and Eve
spanned, who was then the
gentleman?............................*John Balls*
The poor will always
be with us ....*Matthew*
The pheasants are
poor and hungry......................*Wat Tyler*
The angry cat is
poor and hungry.................. *Claude Balls*
Let them do what I did .... *Cornelius
Vanderbilt*
God must have loved the poor, he
made so many of them ....*Abraham
Lincoln*

G 012
Let them eat cupcakes ....*Marie
Antoinette*
Being poor is no sin.........*George Herbert*
Are there no workhouses?..........*Scrooge*
Feed the hungry........................... *Isaiah*
Feed the poor...............................*Jesus*
Keep the poor off my golf
courses...*Trump*
The poor are already
damned ....*John Calvin*
I owe the poor nothing.......... *J.P. Morgan*
Screw the poor........................ *Ayn Rand*

G 013
Hindus who did not follow their caste
rules in previous lives will be born poor
and into low caste families.......*Krishna to
Arjuna*

Religion keeps the poor from
murdering the rich ....*Bonaparte*

H 001
F__k the poor .... *Richard Nixon*
Keep out all the poor people from
"Sh--thole" countries....................*Donald
Drumpf*

H 002
I hear you knocking, but you
can't come in .... *Fats Domino*
St. Peter, don't you call me 'cause I
can't go. I owe my soul to the company
stoe .... *Tennessee Ernie Ford*

H 003
I am the keeper of the Pearly
Gates .... *St. Peter*
I keep track of who's
naughty and nice ....*St. Nicholas*
We will show you where to go.....*Cherubs*
Wait, and let me speak with comrade
God....................*I'm Harry Pollitt, please*

H 004
Wrong place, you are
coming with me............. *The Fallen Angel*
This is the only ferry over
the River Styx ....*Charon*
Watch me jump over this ditch.......... *Evel
Knievel*

Abandon all hope ye who enter
here...*Dante*
Follow me through the
Gates of Hell...................................*Pluto*
Well, I'll be damned....................... *Faust*
That you are .... *Mephistopheles*

H 005
I painted scenes from horrible
dreams of what Hell might look
like .... *Hieronymus Bosch*
Anyone trying to escape,
turn around and
go back, go back, go back.........*Cerberus*
This is my underworld, and who
the Hell are you?.......................... *Osiris*
I'm just been made First People's
Commissar of Soviet Hell ..... *Harry Pollett*

H 006
It's hotter down here than
Vulcan's petzl..........................*Titus Pullo*
Time to turn up all the thermostats
to 666 degrees............................ *Lucifer*
It's hotter than Hell down here ....*Anton*
LaVey
What did you expect?.............. *The Devil*
I think he's expecting a little
professional courtesy..............*The Devil's*
Advocate

H 007
Why do people in Hell always
want ice water?.....................*Old Scratch*
Tell them to stop whining and
complaining........................... *Beelzebub*
No smoking down here
(*cough, cough, cough*)......................*The*
Marlborough Man
More fire and brimstone.......*The Evil One*
Here I am, straight from Brazil.
Any of you read my book,
"*Mein Putz*"? ....*Der Furor*

H 008
No, and you are now going to
the de-lousing showers
down below............................*Der Teufel*
How long must I stay here? ....*Jack the*
Ripper
Look it up in my Devil's
Dictionary...................... *Ambrose Bierce*
Until Hell freezes over .... *Moloch*

H 009
That won't happen until time's end....... *El*
Diablo
I'm told I'm staying here forever ... *Pol Pot*
Me too .... *Idi Amin*
Why me, why me?........ *Heinrich Himmler*
All are staying here
forever................................ *Angra Mainyu*
Time's up, forever starts now..........*Satan*

H 010
We are taking our fire temples and
towers of silence north into Central
Asia....... *Zoroastrian bonfire missionaries*
All virtuous Greeks and Romans may
go to Mt. Parnassos when they
die................................ *Dionysians*

H 011
All good Romans and Greeks may
dance forever in the
Elysian Fields ....*Zorba*
When evil and wicked Greco-Romans
die, they will spend the rest of eternity
in Hades...........................*High priests of*
Rome & Athens

H 012
It's round ....*Eratosthenes*
It's circular .... *Copernicus*
It's elliptical...................................*Kepler*
It moves...................................... *Galileo*
It will fly................................. *Leonardo*
It falls... *Newton*
It's in the water......................*John Snow*
It's alive ....*Frankenstein*

H 013
It pumps .... *Wm. Harvey*
It speaks............................*Alex. G. Bell*
It will go ....*James Watt*
It shines........................ *Thomas Edison*
It flies............................. *Orville & Wilbur*
It flew........................... *Howard Hughes*
It computes....................*Jobs & The Woz*
It prevents.......................*Edward Jenner*

J 001a
The Barnacle Goose is real and it
actually exists in the
North Sea.............*Geraldus Cambrensis*
Plutonic aethers cause bloating in
corpses..........................*Lucius Varenus*

J 001b
Evil humours create most
illnesses................... *Medieval physicians*
Bleeding can cure
illnesses...................... *Medieval barbers*
That sounds like a
midnight snack.......................... *Dracula*

J 002
My book on the ancient Kings of
Britain is absolutely true.......... *Geoffrey of
Monmouth*
The sun goes around the Earth,
anyone can see that....... *Pope Urban VIII*
These leaves are called tobacco and
they will aid in digestion........... *Sir Walter
Raleigh*
It stinks .... *Vernon Wormer*

J 003
Phrenology can reveal people's moral
qualities and intelligence by measuring
bumps on their heads....... *G. & A. Combe*
Piltdown man is real .... *Charles
Dawson*
It is true that, long ago, Hui Shin sailed
his boat from China to Mexico...... *George
Carter*

J 004
Hot climates make people violent,
stupid, slow, and indolent .... *Ellen
Churchill Semple*
Cold climates make people
vigorous, smart, and
industrious .... *Ellsworth Huntington*
Plants and animals that acquire certain
characteristics during their lifetimes
can pass them on to their
offspring......................... *Trofim Lysenko*
Some races are stupider than
others .... *Herrnstein & Murray*
Cold fusion will work.................... *Pons &
Fleischman*
Stressing mouse cells can turn
them into stem cells...................... *Hiroku
Obokata*

J 005
Global warming is real and is caused
primarily by humans............. *Phil Jones &
Michael Mann*
Years ago, ancient Hebrews sailed
across the ocean and settled in
America, and then built lots of Indian
burial mounds......... *The Book of Mormon*

J 006
People who lose a lot of money in a
slot machine will have a greater
chance of winning if they put more
money into the same slot
machine....... *Garden of Allah Casino staff*
Yeah .... *Flamingo Garden Club staff*
I am the owner of the Golden Gate
Bridge, and you can buy it from me
outright for only $1,000.00…You can
give it to me in cash. Just slip it under
my door .... *Brigham Herbalife*

K 001
I will build a great big tower .... *Nimrod*
And we can call it the Great
Erection of Babylon............ *Nabopolassar*
Why can't I understand anything you
Babylonians are saying? ......*Alexander of
Macedon*

K 002
Open the gates for me and all my 40
wives............................... *Joseph Smith*
Open the gates for my 40
thieves....................................... *Ali Baba*
Open sez me .... *Popeye*
Keep the genie in the bottle......... *Aladdin*
Keep sailing the seven seas......... *Sinbad*
Keep staying alive.............. *Saddam Jose*

K 003a
All is natural selection .... *Darwin*
All is historiography................*Ibn Khaldun*
All is natural history...........*von Humboldt*
All is universal history............. *von Ranke*
All is geography ....*Ritter*
All is geographical........................ *Ratzel*

K 003b
All is studying society .... *Max Weber*
All is my geography .... *H.W. van Loon*
All is studying Oreos .... *Nabisco*

K 004
All is studying new topics in history,
such as environmental and
social causal variables .... *Giambattista*
Vico
All is also geographical, economic, and
cultural histories .... *Fernand Braudel*
All is ancient history .... *Herodotus*
All is challenge and response .... *Toynbee*

K 005
All is spatial differentiation ...... *Hartshorne*
All is in decline .... *Spengler*
All is anarchist
geography .... *Élisée Reclus*
All are French landscapes .... *Vidal de la*
Blache
All is theoretical
geography .... *William Bunge*
All is central place theory .... *Christaller*
All are hexagonal land-use
models .... *Losch*
All is the urban concentric ring
model .... *Burgess*
All is the urban sector model .... *Hoyt*
All is the rank-size rule .... *Auerbach*

K 006a
All is the primate
city rule .... *Mark Jefferson*
All is the reverse Burgess
model .... *Schnore*
All is the Isolated state
model .... *von Thunen*
All is the gravity model .... *William Reilly*
All is the principle of least
effort .... *G. K. Zipf*
All is the multiple nuclei model .... *Harris &*
Ullman

K 006b
All is the ice cream vender
model .... *Hotelling*
All is intervening opportunity .... *Stouffer*
All is Cardinal Place analysis .... *Elliott*
All is Buridan's Ass .... *Buridan*

K 007
After we have won the war, we will
relocate huge numbers of good Aryan
families into the eastern lands and
settle them in accordance with the
Christaller central place model and
the Loschian industrial and
retail landscape model .... *General Karl*
Haushofer

K 008
I once wrote a tourist brochure
about my vacation
to Mexico .... *Edward B. Tylor*
Read my book on
chrysanthemums .... *Ruth Benedict*
I studied girls in the South
Pacific .... *Margaret Mead*
All my former graduate stoonts
are Boasians .... *Franz Boas*

K 009
All is suffering .... *Buddha*
All is surreal .... *Dali*
All is bizarre .... *Gaudi*
All is fantasy .... *Disney*
All is genetics .... *Mendel*
All is abstract .... *Picasso*
All is absurd .... *Camus*

K 010
All is rubber .... *Michelin*
All is beer .... *Michelob*
All is tradition .... *Tevya*
All is travel .... *Ibn Battuta*
All is sculpture .... *Michelangelo*
All is drama .... *Aeschylus*
All is printing .... *Gutenberg*
All are quanta .... *Max Planck*
All is random .... *Heisenberg*

K 011

I invented the algebra	*Al-Khwarizmi*
I invented the algebra	*Diophantus*
I invented the calculus	*Newton*
I invented the calculus	*Leibniz*
I invented the calculus	*Ramanujan*

K 012

Please, Brer Bear, don't throw me into that briar patch	*Brer Rabbit*
Open this box, and you'll be sorry	*Pandora*
The sky will be falling	*Chicken Little*
Nobody believes me any more	*Cassandra*
I can predict that there will be rain	*Nostradamus*
I can predict that too, any time	*Edgar Cayce*

K 013

All is love	*St. Valentine*
All is uniform	*Hutton*
All is sequential	*Lyell*
All is adrift	*Wegner*
All is rustica	*Vivaldi*
All is natural beauty	*John Muir*

K 014

All is kindness	*Eleanor Roosevelt*
All is silent	*Rachel Carson*
All is preservation	*Isaac Walton*
All is elementary	*Sherlock*
All is climbing	*Tenzig*
All is not falling	*Mallory*
All is speed	*Usain Bolt*
All is escape	*Houdini*
All is victory	*Patten*
All is illogical	*Spock*

K 015a

Beware the Gordian Knot	*Phrygian Gordium Officiants*

K 015b

Schtup the Gordian Knot	*Iskander*
Beware of Greeks bearing gifts	*Laocoon*
Beware the helots	*Leonidas*
Beware the defenders of Sicily	*Alcibiades*

K 016

Beware of those who have studied only one book	*Thomas Aquinas*
Beware the Ides of March	*The Augur Spurinna*
Beware the Slaves	*Spartacus*
Beware the Teutoburger Forest	*Arminius*
Beware the sword Excalibur	*Merlin*

K 017

Beware the Sword of Damocles	*Cicero*
Beware the headless horseman	*Ichabod*
Beware the horse latitudes	*Magellan*
Beware the Bermuda Triangle	*von Daniken*
Beware the Jabberwock	*Lewis Carroll*
Beware the Kryptonite	*Jor-El*
Beware the Moais of Rapa Nui	*The Kahunas*
Beware the fire and lava	*Pele*
Beware the Ki'eki'e winds	*Kamehameha*
Beware the Sandwich Isle Luaus	*Capt. Cook*
Beware the Frozen Chosen	*G.I's in Korea*
Come see my oceanic raft	*Thor Heyerdahl*

K 018

Scholars in the west should be studying Greco-Roman and Arabic math, science, and astronomy. There is much to learn	*Pope Sylvester II*

K 019
They eat spaghetti just
like us .... *Marco Polo*
It's safer to be feared than
loved...................................*Machiavelli*
Here is something to drink .... *Lucrezia*
Borgia
No thanks .... *Nickelodeon de Medici*
Paint according to nature and
reality.. *Giotto*
What a wonderful idea...............*Raphael*

K 020
When the moon hits your eye
lika big pizza pie,
at's amore............................*Dean Martin*
Three coins in the
fountain............................ *The Four Aces*
Que será, será .... *Doris Day*
Best canned spaghetti and meatballs in
da whole south Bronx.......*Chef Boyardee*
Come to Coney Island...............*Nathan's*

K 021
Make him an offer he can't
refuse ....*Don Vito Corleone*
Come wis me to da casbah............. *Rudy*
Valentino
See? It's just
business ....*Michael Corleone*
We're bigger than U.S. Steel.......... *Meyer*
Lansky
The movie was just as good .... *Mario*
Puzo
Tax evasion? Mamma Mía!......*Al Capone*

L 001
Fascism will make Italy great
again .... *Mussolini*
That's precisely what Trump said about
America last week....................*Anderson*
Cooper
Trump talks like Mussolini, but governs
like Mr. Bean......................*Dana Milbank*

L 002
We've come here to teach
you people Arabic ....*Tariq ibn-Ziad*
The Reconquista begins in
Asturias .... *Reccared*
Estoy montando en mí
caballo muerto ...... *Rodrigo Díaz de Bivar*

L 003
We will fund your expedition over the
ocean sea west to
the Indies................ *Isabella & Ferdinand*
In fourteen-hundred and ninety-two, I
did sail the ocean blue, and the Indies
are ours.................................. *Columbus*
Hoo-ah .... *Al Pacino*

L 004
After the beginning, the Mayan
Long Count calendar
was created .... *Mayan sages*
Long ago, there were the Zapotecs
(people of the clouds) and the nearby
and closely related Mixtecs (people of
the rain). Together, they rose up onto
the surface of the Valley of Oaxaca
from underground caverns and then
built the city of Monte Alban...... *Mixtecs &*
Zapotecs

L 005
In the beginning was the creator god in
the form of the feathered serpent,
Quetzalcoatl..... *Sacredots of Teotihuacan*

L 006
After the beginning, the sun god Inti
raised up the ancestors of the
Quechua people out of Lake Titicaca
and onto the surface of
the Altiplano....................*Inca sacerdotes*

L 007
After the beginning was the
hermaphrodite god Ometecuhtli-
Omecihuatl, along with the sun god
Huitzilopochtli, who sent the Nahuatl
people south from Aztlan to Lake
Texcoco in the Valley of Anahuac ... *Aztec
sacerdotes*

L 008
Africa begins at the
Pyrenees .... *Napoleon*
I can see in the distance un molino de
viento .... *Don Quixote*
The French soldiers lined up our
villagers and shot them all .... *El Greco*
The Germans bombed our
villages .... *Picasso*
The Civil War is over, and I am now
Caudillo de España and Jefe de
Estado .... *Francisco Franco*

L 009
I was the first Russian tsar ..... *Rurik of the
Varangians*
I am the most feared tsar
of all the Russias .... *John Terrible*

L 010
Burn your kaftans and cut
off your beards. That goes for all
Boyars .... *Peter the Great*
Now watch me as I build Russia's
first sailing ship .... *Санкт-Петербург*
I am bringing in hundreds of families
from Germany who will build
agricultural settlements along the
Volga River .... *Catherine the Great*
I am freeing all the
serfs .... *Czar Alexander II*
The Czar has been assassinated .... *Court
herald*
No good turns ever go
unpunished .... *Gogol & Dostoevsky*

L 011
Scratch a Russian, find
a Tatar .... *Marquis de Cuisine*
It does not really
take a village .... *Potemkin*
I can heal the czardine .... *Rasputin*
War is always started
by rulers .... *Tolstoy*

L 012
Thesis, antithesis, sisyphus .... *Hegel*
Religion is the opium of the people .... *Karl*
Work is the curse of the laboring
class .... *Engels*
Say da magic woid and win 25
rubles .... *Groucho*
What is not to be done .... *Lenin*
Yes, this is more just .... *Zhivago*
Oh, no they shot the Czar .... *Kulaks*
There's no turning back .... *Party
apparatchiks*
How many divisions does the
pope have? .... *Josef Dzhugashvili*

L 013
We defeated the supermen at
Stalingrad and at Kursk, and then
drove them back into
the snow to die .... *Marshal Zhukov*

L 014
Stalin was a monster ..... *Nikita Khruschev*
First Russian in space .... *Yuri Gagarin*
In America you can always find a party,
in Russia, party always
finds you .... *Yakov Smirnoff*

L 015
If we let them, will they
leave? .... *Gorbachev*
More vodka! .... *Boris Yeltsin*
Don't I look dashing riding
bareback? .... *Putin*

L 016

We have taken Constantinople, and it's
now called Istanbul................. *Mehmed II*
I have the world's
largest turban.....................*Suleiman the
Magnificent*
Come and see the wonderful
Turkish Baths in Istanbul .....*Jean Ingress*

L 017

Our children couldn't read Arabic, so
now we are teaching them to read
using the Latin alphabet...............*Ataturk*
Burn your fez's and cut
off your *!u*^! x beards .....*Mustafa Kemal*
And you can't go back to
Constantinople........................*Nat Simon*

L 018

We beat off the Turks at
the siege of Vienna........ *John III Sobieski*
We defeated the Turkish fleet at the
Battle of Lepanto.............*John of Austria*
I financed the
battle of Lepanto ....*Pope Pius V*

L 019

Napoleon is gone and Europe is
now safe from democracy........*Metternich*
The Pope ordered me to stop
studying garden peas.......*Gregor Mendel*
I'd like to pay a nice friendly
visit to Sarajevo............. *Franz Ferdinand*
Edelweiss, edelweiss..........*Trapp Family
singers*

M 001

Ich haben ein few suggestions.......*Martin
Luther*
Toujours l'audace.....................*Frederick
der Grosse*
Ich bin der beste.........................*Mozart*
Dit dit dit dah.........................*Beethoven*

M 002a

Deutschland uber alles.............*Bismarck*
Die Valkyries sind Deutschland....*Wagner*

M 002b

Prussian Glory March........*Johann Piefke*
Ich bin der rote baron.............*Richthofen*
Ich retired to mein estate in
Holland...................................*Wilhelm II*

M 003

Whenever Ich hear das word
Kultur, Ich reach for mein
revolver ....*Hermann Goering*
Ich habe only
eine ball...................... *Schmecklegruber*
Ich habe zwei, but eine iss
schmall.......................................*Goering*
Ich habe zwei, but eine iss
similar...*Himmler*
Und Ich haben nicht at all.........*Goebbels*
Und Ich never had
any to start with at all ....*Axis Sally*
Ich bin der Wustenfux ....*Rommel*
Ich hate all diss +@%# snow.....*Guderian*
You ain't nothing but
a schweinhund...................................*Elvis*

M 004

Ve vill name our new V-2 rocket
"das fire-geschpittin-
geschnorten".........................*Albert Speer*
In German und English, Ich learned
to count down, und Ich learning
Chinese, says........... *Wherner von Braun*

M 005

During der Grosse War ve engaged
die British at Jutland........ *Admiral Scheer*
Das Boot iss home und ve
are now safe.... *Captain-Lieutenant Lehm*
Mein Wehrmacht ist kaput, und ve are
surrendering ....*Field Marshal Paulus*
Der Bismarck is listing to
port, pull das plug............*Admiral Lutjens*
Der Graf spee iss doomed,
pull das plug ....*Admiral Langsdorf*
Der Schornhorst has capsized and
is going down............*Kapitan Fritz Hintze*
Any port in a storm.......*Popeye der sailor
mensch*

M 006
Vere doss Ich signen?..... *Admiral Donuts*
On the dotted line.....*General Eisenhower*
We will now begin trying all Nazis for
crimes against humanity.... *Harry Truman*
After many years, it now takes zwei
hands to hold ein Vopper........*Der Burger
Koenig*

M 007
We lost everything..............*Vercingetorix*
Not to worry. Every month, a comic
book is printed in Paris that shows how
we won most battles against the
Romans.......................*Asterix the Gaul*

M 008
In seven thirty-two at Tours, I myself
defeated the Moors .... *Charles Martel*
Liberté, Egalité, Sororité ....*Joan Dark*

M 009
The sewers of Paris aren't as bad as
they say. They are really just...
less miserable.....................*Jean Valjean*
Arrete curé et ecraser l'infâme .....*Voltaire*
Of noble sausages ....*Rousseau*
Our laws, c'est la France .....*Montesquieu*
Come see our painting of the
Burglars of Calais..........*Rodin & Moeglin*

M 010
L'etat, c'est moi ....*Louis XIV*
Apres moi le deluge....................*Louis XV*
Apres moi le reign of terror ....*Louis XVI*
Off with their heads! ....*Robespierre*
Arrete la guillotine! ....*Danton*
A Marat....................*Jaques-Louie David*
I'm starting a new custom for all French
men – bathe every day ....*Beau Brummell*

M 011
Je suis pas merde in un silk
stocking...............................*Talleyrand*
Yes you are ....*Napoleon I*
L'empire, c'est grand...........*Napoleon III*
J'accuse ....*Emile Zola*
M 011b
I will call them germs...................*Pasteur*
A bas la Peste ....*Camus*

M 012
Vive les Boches ....*Petain*
Je suis la France.....................*de Gaulle*
Je ne vinaigrette rien...............*Edith Piaf*
Thank heaven for little girls.........*Maurice
Chevalier*

M 013
Sur le Pont d'Avignon on y dance.....*Fred
Astaire*
Nous ne danse pas .....*Francois Hollande*
Yes oui can................*Emmanuel Macron*
I was the pope of French Cuisine......*Paul
Bocuse*

Non, nous n'allons
pas y ....*Les Medecins Avec Frontieres*

M 014
Voodoo is real and keeps
people in line .... *Papa Doc Duvalier*
Santeria is also real and
quite useful................ *Baby Doc Duvalier*
I was president for life .... *Jean-Bedel
Bokassa*

N 001
Something is rotten in Denmark.......*Saxo
Grammaticus*
We frequently vacationed to the
east coast of England..........*Eric Bloodax*
We now control all of Briton north and
east of Watling Street, in the
Danelaw ....*King Guthrum*
England and Denmark are
now one.........................*Cnut the Great*

N 002
I took the first Norse settlers to Iceland
in the year 874 .... *Ingolfr Arnarson*
Irish monks were already
there .... *Carl Sauer*
We also sailed west from Norway and
settled in Iceland .... *Eric the Red*
Several years later, we traveled to
Greenland and then
to Vinland.............................*Leif Ericson*

N 003
The Little Mermaid lives.... *Hans Christian*
                                            Anderson
The Huns are now our friends ..... *Quisling*
We sank the German battle cruiser
Tirpitz in a Norwegian Fjord .... *The RAF*

N 004
Oboes sound like clarinets
with the croup...................... *Victor Borge*
I once spent a year communing
with nature in New Mexico .... *Niels Bohr*
We've come to fish for the herring
fish that live in this
beautiful sea .... *Winkin, Blinkin, & Nod*
I can't get my finger out of this
+*p*#!]$ dike .... *Hans Brinker*

N 005
Everyone will get rich buying and
selling these tulip bulbs .... *The Dutch*
                                    Stock Exchange
De Vliegende Hollander
will fly on forever .... *KLM*

N 006a
I discovered the Tappan Zee in New
Netherlands and the river, which I
named for myself............... *Henry Hudson*
We bought Manhattan Island
from the Indians for a few guilders
worth of junk and trinkets ...... *Peter Minuit*

N 006b
Then we built the city of New
Amsterdam on the southern tip
of the island .... *Peter Stuyvesant*

N 007
Later, British ships came and gently
persuaded us to lower our flag and
then took over our city and
renamed it New York................. *Governor*
                                            Stuyvesant
We still have a nice little
Dutch village here in
the Catskills .... *Katrina Van Tassel*
Everything here is now well-organized,
tidy, and spic & span............... *The Dutch*
                                    Cleanser Girl

N 008
All snakes be gone.................. *St. Patrick*
Many people have a nationality, but the
Irish have a psychosis ..... *Brendan Behan*
After death, Tir na nOg (land of eternal
youth) awaits for all virtuous and sober
Irishmen to enter........ *Ancient Irish druids*
I had many adventures, and then was
killed after tying myself to a standing
stone .... *Cu Chuchulainn*
                                    (koo-kullan)

N 009
After many quests, I went into a cave
and went to sleep, and someday I'll
wake up and come back to defend
Ireland .... *Finn MacCummail*
                                    (finn mc-kool)

N 010
We are staying in Dublin and
will call our settlement
Ostmantown .... *Norse Vikings*
There goes the neighborhood...... *Dermait*
                                    Mac Murrough
I'm the dish with the fish ...... *Molly Malone*
I'm the floozie in the jacuzzi..... *Anna Livia*

N 011
Work is the curse of the
drinking class .... *Oscar Wilde*
Too many Irishmen die of the dark, and
the damp, and the drink .... *Frank McCourt*
bejayzzus/dalpmfinn/bnb/byob ...... *James
Joyce*
Come watch the 130th national
Hurling Championship
in Dublin ....*Gaelic Athletic
Association*

P 001
We want to teach you Britons
Latin .... *Suetonius*
Not without a fight, gobshita ...... *Boadicea*
Remember the Battle of Mons
Graupius, where the Picts under
Calgacus fought off the Romans under
Julius Agricola........................... *Tacitus*
This wall will keep the marauding Picts
out of Roman Britain...................*Hadrian*

P 002
Remember the Battle of Mons Badon,
where the Roman Britons fought off the
invading Saxons.......................... *Bede*
I can't stand all this noise........... *Grendel*
Come hear my classical Rendition of
Beowulf..............................*Julian Glover*
We've come here to help you keep out
the Irish and German
raiders ....*Hengist & Horsa*
These cakes taste horrible........*Alfred the
Great*

P 003
Fæder ure, þu þe eart on
heofonum.......................... *Offa of Mercia*
Get back, back I say!.....*Canute the Dane*
I defenestrated the foul wretch ... *Edward I*
Oh no! Piers Gaveston was my
best and only friend................. *Edward II*

P 004
To Canterbury they wende, the holy
blissful martir for
to seke .... *Geoffrey Chaucer*
You may call me Bubbles ...... *The Wife of
Bath*
Put your clothes back on, wife ...... *Leofric
the Dane*

P 005
We've come to teach you French.
Swine will become pork, sheep will
become mutton, calf will become veal,
chicken will become poultry, cow will
become beef, a drink will become a
beverage, wine will become vin, and
deer will become venison ..... *Guillaume of
Normandy*

P 006
Remember we were here on Saint
Crispin's Day. And now,
once more onto the beach.......... *Henry V*
I don't like wars, they have uncertain
outcomes, but we did destroy the
Spanish Armada
rather nicely............. *Elizabeth The Great*
Bard of Avon calling ....*Shakespeare*

P 007
Anyone going to Scarborough Fair?
Which road will you be taking? .... *Dick
Turpin*
Going through Nottinghamshire? Stop
and chat for a while...............*Robin Hood*

P 008
Ring around the rosies, a pocket full of
posies, atchoo, atchoo, we all fall down
(dead). It's Time........ *The Angel of Death*
Bring out your dead............ *Monty Python*
That's what happens when the plague
comes around.............. *The Grim Reaper*

P 009
Yes, we will come............*Mary & Wm. of Orange*
It's a long way to Tipperary.......*William of Orange*
I will be the last English king to lead troops into battle, and we will defeat the Jacobites at the Battle of the Boyne.....................................*William III*
Get out of my way, and get me to France, right now! ....James II

P 010
We lost all at Culloden.... *Charles Edward Stuart*
MacDonalds and Campbells have been feuding with each other for centuries........................*Sir Walter Scott*

P 011
It's called tobacco........ *Sir Walter Raleigh*
Get rid of that stinking weed................... *James I Stuart*
Scribble, scribble, scribble, eh Mr. Gibbon? .... *King James I & VI*
Whenever men of business get together, they immediately begin to conspire against the public good.....*Adam Smith*
Patriotism is the last refuge of the scoundrel .... *Dr. Samuel Johnson*

P 012
Knowledge is power..........*Francis Bacon*
Knowledge is good.................*Emil Faber*
We don't need no edjukaytion, and we don't need no thought control ......*Pink Floyd*

P 013a
Human happiness consists in action, pleasure, and indolence........*David Hume*

P 013b
Ya canna be both grand and comfortable........................*Rabbie Burns*
That German in London took away my family name .... *Rob Roy MacGregor*
Wee Doch-An'-Doris and Roamin in the Gloamin, and Guinness is good for you........................*Harry Lauder*
Bond, James Bond............*Sean Connery*

P 014
I'm sending an army to America to remind the Loyalists of my love...............................*George III*
We destroyed the Spaniards at Trafalgar..................*Admiral Lord Nelson*
Oh, I've seen Boney's back before........................ *Duke of Wellington*
The world has turned upside down, and we had to return earlier than I had planned ....*General Cornwallis*

P 015
Let me help put out this little fire ....*Charles II*
Does anyone remember how many times the Thames froze up?......... *Queen Victoria*

P 016
There's a lot of money to be made in India (opium and tea)........... *British East India Co.*
Also in China and Singapore (opium, tea, and silk)....*Jardine Matheson & Co.*
Also in Canada (furs and timber).................*Hudson Bay Company*
Also in Jamaica and the Caribbean (rum, sugar, and slaves).... *Henry Morgan*
Also in South Africa (gold, cattle, and diamonds)................... *Cecil Rhodes*
The pigeons up here are really a bit messy................................. *Lord Nelson*
More punishment until morale improves................................ *Capt. Bligh*

P 017
Come mister tally man, tally me
banana. Daylight come and me wan go
home…Work, work, work Senora, work
your body lina.................*Harry Belafonte*
What a hell of a way to end a
career....................................*Usain Bolt*

P 018
Eliminate unnecessary entities in
seeking what is real and
what isn't........................ *Wm. of Ockham*
World population will multiply
faster than world food supply ...... *Thomas
Malthus*
Only the fittest survive ... *Herbert Spencer*
Britain must abolish the
slave trade................ *William Wilberforce*

Q 001
Those who control the seas
control the world................. *Themistocles*
Those who control Messina
control Sicily............................*Alcibiades*

Q 002
Those who control the heartland
control the world.....................*Mackinder*
Those who control the rimland
control the world...................... *Spykman*
Those who control the past
control the future.............. *George Orwell*
I've seen the future, and
it's not very good.................... *H.G. Wells*

Q 003
Those who control the high ground
control the world............ *Lynden Johnson*
Those who control the newspapers
control the politicians...... *Rupert Murdoch*
Those who control the media
control the world............... *George Soros*
Those who have the money will
control the media.............. *The Koch Bros.*

Q 004
We will attack directly into the machine
gun fire and win this war by
attrition…and I will
not be there .... *Field Marshal
Douglas Haig*
Gallipoli was a disaster......*ANZAC troops*
We've taken Aqaba... *Lawrence of Arabia*
What am I supposed to do with
Damascus? .... *General Allenby*
You can give it to the Arabs.............. *T.E.
Lawrence*

Q 005
Today, many British cathedrals have
hundreds of wooden shutters along
their inside walls with thousands of
names inscribed on them for those who
died in the trenches of the war to end
all wars (i.e., Salisbury Cathedral) ... *HME*

Q 006
Chariots of Fire ....*Vangelis*
I won an Olympic gold
medal in Paris.............. *Harold Abrahams*
So did I.................................... *Eric Liddell*
I also won a medal in
the 1924 Olympics .... *Jackson Scholz*
I did too ....*Charles Paddock*
I was the first to break the
four-minute mile.............. *Roger Bannister*
I broke it too........................... *John Landy*

Q 007a
Come out to Africa, young man, and
help pick up the white man's
burden..............................,... *Cecil Rhodes*
Dr. Livingstone, I presume?....... *Henry M.
Stanley*

Bingo Bango Bongo, I don't wanna
leave the Congo.............*David Livingston*
Come ye back, ye British soldier,
come ye back
to Mandalay.....................*Rudyard Kipling*

Q 007b
On the Road to Mandalay............ *Hope &*
Crosby
Go west young man ....*Horace Greeley*
I was president for life................ *Idi Amin*
I was president for life...... *Robert Mugabe*

Q 008
Speak with the animals........... *St. Francis*
Talk to your garden plants .... *Prince*
Jughead
Talk to the animals .... *Dr. Dolittle*
Come on Dovah, come on boy,
move yer bloomin arse! ...... *Eliza Doolittle*

Q 009
We must preserve the British Navy's
most cherished traditions........ *The British*
Admiralty
What traditions? You must mean rum,
sodomy, and the lash? .... *Churchill*
Mr. Churchill, if I were your wife, I'd
put poison in your brandy ..... *Lady Ashley*
Madam, if I were your husband
I'd drink it .... *Winston Churchill*

Q 010
Peace in our time ..... *Neville Chamberlain*
Never, never, ever give up......... *Churchill*
Imagine me sitting on a mine
on the Maginot Line......... *George Formby*
Sink the Bismarck .... *British Admiralty*
I chased Rommel all the way across
North Africa.... *Field Marshal Montgomery*

Q 011a
Please send us more of your
nice ten-pound Poms.............. *Australian*
Immigration authorities
You'll come a Waltzing Matilda
with me.......................... *Banjo Patterson*
Tie me kangaroo down,
sport ....*Rolph Harris*
Any roo meat in
Big Macs here? .... *Aussie meat &*
carrion Inspectors
Oh no, not yet I hope.................. *Skippy*

Q 011b
First Kiwi to the top of
Mt. Everest .... *Hillary & Tenzing*

Q 012
We still have possession
of the Ashes......................... *The Botany*
Bay Growlers
All dingoes go to
dingo heaven ....*Dame Edna*

Q 013
There was something to be proud of
when Australia's first mass-produced
car rolled off the assembly line almost
70 years ago, and I named it the
Holden.........................*James A. Holden*

Q 014
Long ago is in what we call the
Dreaming Time .... *Aust. Aborigines*
Many of us also call ourselves Koories.
The didgeridoo has been our people's
instrument for over 40,000 years ..... *Djalu*
Gurruwiwi

Q 015
I was the last of the Tasmanian
Aborigines in Australia....... *Twi, Truganini*
After 60,000 years, does the Uluru
agreement mean we will
get to vote?.............. *Abos of northern Oz*

R 001
At the beginning, there was Gitche
Manitou, who existed everywhere and
rules over everything...... *Chichimec tribal*
shamans
At the beginning was Tawa, who raised
up all peoples from the underworlds
and scattered them to the four
winds...................... *Spider Grandmother*
After death, the spirits of skillful
warriors and hunters can spend
eternity in the Happy
Hunting Ground .... *Many Horses of the*
Lakota Sioux

R 002
Long ago, there were many of these
mound settlements. At different times,
there were between 20,000 to 40,000
people living in this particular city,
located east of the Mississippi and
north of the Ohio .... *The Great Chief of
Cahokia Mounds*

R 003
Many years ago, there were between
4,000 and 6,000 people living in this
great settlement on the southern
Mississippi. A large band of white
soldiers came by, and then most
of our people died of the spotted
disease .... *The Great Sun of the
Natchez Mounds*

R 004
Everything in the Indies is
ours .... *Columbus*
We never found the
Fountain of Youth .... *Hernando deSoto*
We were never able find any gold or
the seven cities of Cibola .... *Cabeza de
Vaca*
My expedition didn't find
anything either .... *Coronado*

R 005
We'll make a road, called the El
Camino Real, and we will establish
missions along it that the Indians
will build as they learn
to love Jesus .... *Junipero Serra*

R 006a
We've come to teach you Spanish and
all about encomienda .... *Cortez &
Pizarro*

R 006b
Caca de toro, cabrón .... *Montezuma*
Please leave us alone .... *Atahualpa*

R 007
Awright, you can have
#*^@! Tejas .... *Santa Anna*
I was the first Indio
Prez of Mexico .... *Benito Juarez*
We don't need no steenking
badges .... *Pancho Villa*
My name Jose Jimenez .... *Bill Dana*
How are things in Guacamole? .... *Pedro
O'Reilly*
Vaya con carne .... *Cantinflas*
All the world loves
Gordo Lopez .... *Gus Arriola*
You're in Hernando's Hideaway .... *Olé*

R 008
No llores por mí, Argentina ..... *Eva Duarte
Perón*
All the world loves Evita .... *Juan Perón*

R 009
We settled our first colony on Roanoke
Island, and then could not resupply
them on account of the Spanish
Armada .... *Amadas & Barlowe*
When we returned to the island,
everyone was gone .... *Richard Grenville*

R 010
Several years later, we founded
another settlement in the Virginia
Colony located on the
James River .... *Sir Walter Raleigh*
These English chose a bad place to
settle. The water is not good, they also
stink .... *Powhatan*
We are starving, maybe the Indians will
give us some food .... *John Smith*
Father, please let him go ...... *Pocahontas*

R 011
Several years later, we founded the
Plymouth Colony farther north
and other colonies followed .... *William*
Brewster
Bury a fish with the maize, beans,
and squash seeds .... *Squanto*
Help us against our enemies ...... *Samoset*
We are friends of the Plymouth
Pilgrims .... *Massasoit*

R 012
I am an Iroquois and was not born on
the shores of Gitchee Gummee. All
Indians must unite into one
nation .... *Hiawatha*
We must unite to keep our
lands .... *Tecumseh*

R 013
I discovered Vinland and founded a
settlement there at L'anse aux
Meadows. But there were
too many hostile Skrælings, and we
had to go back to
Greenland .... *Leif Ericson*

R 014
I brought in many French settlers from
France and planted them in Quebec
and Acadia .... *Champlain*

R 015
I also claimed all the territories west of
the Appalachians for France .... *La Salle*
When the French lost the war with the
British, many French Acadians were
exiled to Louisiana where they became
known as Cajuns .... *Evangeline*
Some stayed in Acadia and were
hidden by neighboring
families .... *NS Museum attendants*

R 016
After 1812, many French living west of
the Appalachians crossed the
Mississippi and founded the city
of St. Louis .... *Amable Huge*
I didn't cremate Sam McGee .... *Robert*
Service

R 017
Mush, you
Huskies .... *Sgt. Preston of the Yukon*
Don't build houses on top of the
muskeg .... *RCMP building Inspectors*
Come see our sunsets .... *Heywood &*
Williams

R 018
I scored hat-tricks well into
my 50s .... *Gordie Howe*
Come to my restaurant
in Toronto .... *Wayne Gretzky*
Thirty-three Stanley Cups pour
Les Habs de Montreal ...... *Justin Trudeau*
OK, guys, get out there on the ice and
stay out of the
penalty box .... *Paul Newman*
What did he just say? .... *The Hanson*
Brothers

S 001
All witches must be rounded
up and dealt with .... *Cotton Mather*
What? We have no laws in
Pennsylvania against women riding on
broomsticks, so up thine and get thy
sorry ass out of my
beloved colony .... *William Penn*

S 002
The English are coming!
The English are coming! .... *Paul Revere*
Comte de Grasse's French fleet kept
the Royal Navy away from
Yorktown .... *Lafayette*
The world turned
upside down .... *Cornwallis*

S 003
We should never have sacked Toronto.
They just burned down the
White House ....*James Madison*
To Anacreon in
heaven.........................*Francis Scott Key*

S 004a
In 1814, we took a little trip, along
with Colonel Jackson down the
mighty Mississip.............. *Johnny Horton*
We fired our cannons and they began
to running, down the Mississippi to
the Gulf of Mexico ....*Jean Lafitte*
Old Man River, he just
keeps rolling along ....*Paul Robeson*

S 004b
Napoleon wants to sell us all the
French territories west of the
Mississippi .... *Thomas Jefferson*
This river goes on forever........... *Lewis &*
Clark

The ocean is just over the
next mountain ....*Sacajawea*

S 004c
Y'all can go to hell,
I'm going to Texas............. *Davy Crockett*
His decision, let him enforce it ....*Andy*
Jackson
Tippecanoe and Tyler too .... *Wm. H.*
Harrison
Remember the Alamo.........*Sam Houston*
Fifty-four forty or fight ....*James K. Polk*
I'd rather be right
than president.......................*Henry Clay*

S 004d
Gold is discovered at Sutter's Mill, and
everyone can come to my store in San
Francisco and buy lots of food,
supplies, and gold equipment ......*Samuel*
Brannon

S 005a
The tourist brochures didn't say
there might be some snow blocking
this pass.....................*The Donner Party*
What's for supper?............. *Alferd Packer*

S 005b
I'm moldering in my grave .....*John Brown*
Be there fustis with the mostest ...*General*
N.B. Forrest
At Bull Run, the Feds ran away,
and so did we ....*Spectators from DC*
Here at Gettysburg, the Union line will
break in the middle.............*Robert E. Lee*

S 005c
Turn the guns around..................*General*
Armistead
Let's go, Wolverines..... *George A. Custer*
BAYONETS!........... *Joshua Chamberlain*

S 005d
They ain't a-coming....,*General Longstreet*
General Lee,
I have no division............ *General Pickett*
It's all my fault......................*General Lee*
The enemy is driven
from our soil.................... *General Meade*

S 006a
Hit 'em again and again...........*Ulysses S.*
Grant
Atlanta went up rather well ....*Wm. T.*
Sherman
We are here to surrender the
southern forces....................*General Lee*
Your men can keep their horses. They
will need them when they go home for
the spring planting............. *General Grant*

S 006b
When Johnny comes
marching home .... *Patrick Gilmore*
Oh, you haven't an arm, you haven't a
leg, you're a hopeless, helpless,
shapeless egg, and you'll have to sit
with a bowl and beg. Oh, Johnny, I
hardly knew ya .... *Joan Baez*
Oh captain, my captain ...... *Walt Whitman*

S 006c
I came in with Halley's Comet, and I
hope to go out with it, too .... *Mark Twain*
We're drifting along with the tumbling
tumbleweeds .... *Sons of the Pioneers*
I'm an old cowhand from the Rio
Grande .... *Roy Rogers*
Out in the west Texas town of El Paso,
I fell in love with a Mexican girl .... *Marty
Robbins*
Don't forsake me,
oh my darling .... *Frankie Laine*

S 017a
Don't bring your guns
to town .... *Wyatt Earp*
Get up on your horse and get out of
Dodge, and take your guns with
you .... *Marshall Dillon*
And the horse you rode in on .... *Brando*

S 017b
All God's chilluns gots to
have a gun .... *Smith & Wesson*
Guns are good for you .... *NRA*
Don't bring your guns
to town .... *Wyatt Earp*
From my cold, dead hands! .... *Charlton
Heston*
Nah, you'll shoot your eye out .... *Santa
Claus*

S 017c
Where's the best place to stay in this
town? .... *Doc Holliday*
You can stay in my Long Branch
Saloon. We've got the best bar,
kitchen, gambling den, and whore
house in Kansas .... *Miss Kitty*
I really did love that role .... *Amanda Blake*

S 017d
Poachers shot most of our buffalo
and took away their hides ...... *Kicking Bird*
I shot hundreds of buffalo out
on the northern
Great Plains .... *William F. Cody*
Texas Rangers shot all
of our horses .... *Quana Parker*
Custer had it coming .... *Crazy Horse*
Yellow Hair shot himself .... *Sitting Bull*

S 017e
Join our Ghost Dance and wear these
magic shirts that will ward off bullets
fired by soldiers .... *Wewoka*

S 018a
Stop shooting, we're friends .. *Black Kettle*
I will fight no more .... *Chief Joseph*
Bury my heart at
Wounded Knee .... *Spotted Elk*
I am the last of
my people .... *Ishi of the Yana*
They took away my
Olympic medals .... *Jim Thorpe*
I helped plant the flag at
Mount Suribachi on Iwo Jima .... *Ira Hayes*

S 018b
I retired to my Florida estate
on Key Mosabe .... *Jay Silverheels*
Welcome to our new casino
overlooking the Pacific Ocean in
Washington .... *Chief Quinault*
Welcome to our hotel and
casino at Fort Hall,
Idaho .... *Shoshone-Bannock
Tribe*

S 019
We finally completed the Trans-Atlantic
telegraph cable .... *Cyrus W. Field*
dit dah/ dah dit dit/ dit dit dah dit
(earlier distress call) .... *Samuel Morse*
Sorry, you dialed the wrong
number .... *Alexander Graham Bell*
dit dit dit/ dah dah dah/ dit dit dit
(new universal distress call) .... *S. Morse*

S 020
Remember the Maine ...... *Joseph Pulitzer*
You provide the ships, and I'll provide
the war.............. *William Randolph Hearst*
Play my theme song............. *Garry Owen*
It was a splendid little war .... *John Hay*
Stars and stripes forever......... *John Philip*
Sousa

S 021a
And we won't be back 'til
it's over over there................ *Irving Berlin*
All my men are as clean
as a whistle...................... *Gen. Pershing*
We will fight in France as independent
units under U.S. command ..... *Black-Jack*
Pershing
Hands up, now git .... *Sgt. Alvin York*
I shot down 26 Fokkers .... *Eddie*
Rickenbacker
I got a nasty whiff of poison
gas over there........... *Christy Mathewson*

S 021b
This train will be a
little late .... *Jesse James*
Use enough dynamite
there, Butch? .... *Sundance*
This is a bank robbery,
hands up........................ *Bonnie & Clyde*
Because that's where
the money is .... *Willie Sutton*
Dillinger now has a few more holes
in him than he used to .... *Melvin Purvis*

S 021c
I was once the best hoofer
on Broadway............ *Bojangles Robinson*
I wrote and played "The Entertainer" on
the piano .... *Scott Joplin*

S 021d
Everything is in the Jungle..... *Frank Buck*
Everything is a good
landing .... *Lucky Lindy*
Everything is just fine ...... *Calvin Coolidge*

S 021e
Away, away with
rum, by gum........................ *Carrie Nation*
I outran the Huns in Berlin............. *Jesse*
Owens
During prohibition, many of
us got very rich .... *Joe Kennedy*

S 022a
New York, New York. The Bronx is up
and the Battery's down.... *Frank Sinatra &*
Gene Kelly

S 022b
My constituents can't read, but
it's those damn cartoons that give
me heartburn .... *Boss Tweed*
Everyone in New York City is Jewish,
even if they aren't Jewish ... *Rudy Giuliani*

S 022c
We all grew up here in New York
City....... *Gummo, Chico, Zeppo, & Minnie*
Say da magic woid and win a hundred
dollars .... *Groucho Marx*
Beep beep........................... *Harpo Marx*
We're not related to Karl..... *Marx brothers*

S 023
Chicago, Chicago, that toddlin'
town .... *Sinatra*
Do you know the way to San
Jose? .... *Dionne Warwick*
Gary Indiana........ *Robert Preston & Ron*
Howard

S 024
I took an ax and gave my
parents forty whacks ....*Lizzie Borden*
I didn't wash my hands,
sorry about that.................*Typhoid Mary*
We got trouble right
here in River City................*Professor Hill*
I'm mad as hell and I'm not going
to take it any more.............*Albert Finney*

S 025
I'm opening a new opera house in
downtown Denver ....*Baby Doe Tabor*
I'm unsinkable.....................*Molly Brown*
I am leaving Denver and am
emigrating to Israel................*Golda Meir*
Mazel tov ....*May, Daniels,*
& Fisher families

T 001
Episcopalians have all the pageantry
and none of the guilt.........*Robin Williams*
Onward Christian Soldiers .. *Elmer Gantry*
Methodists are Baptists
who can read ....*Rev. Maclean*
Presbyterians are Methodists who
have money ....*Father Guido*
Time is money............. *Benjamin Franklin*
Greed is good .... *Gordon Gekko*
God loves rich people........... *Joel Osteen*

T 002
Illnesses are illusions that can be
cured by prayer and faith .... *Mary Baker*
Eddy
I've cured many sick, lame, blind, deaf,
and insane people............... *Amy Semple*
McPherson
More lepers? Oy............. *Mother Theresa*
I once saw a 300-foot-tall apparition of
Jesus Christ in downtown
Tulsa ....*Anal Roberts*
I was pretty good as a
child evangelist ....*Marjoe Gortner*

T 003
Several millions of years ago, there
were dinosaurs living at
the same time as human
beings .... *Jim & Tammy Bakker,*
Jerry Foulwell,
Jimmy Swaggart,
Pat Robertson

T 004
In Kentucky, I built a full-size replica of
Noah Zark, along with true-to-life
replicas of cows, worms, giraffes,
ducks, roaches, fish, buzzards,
dinosaurs, butterflies, muttons,
mammoths, dogs & cats, hyenas,
snakes, rats, and wild Indians.....*Kenneth*
Ham
Dinos? No way. And hey, I should
know more about all this stuff
than any of these turkeys .....*Trevor Noah*

T 005
The original Ku Klux Klan was a social
fraternity dedicated to the
betterment of Southern
society................ *Nathan Bedford Forrest*
We both refused to sit in the
back of the bus .... *Jackie Robinson &*
Rosa Parks
We integrated whites-only lunch
counters in Birmingham........*M.L. King Jr.*

T 006
Segregation today, tomorrow, and next
week .... *George Wallace*
Yeah, that's my kid, but don't
tell anyone.................... *Strom Thurmond*
We ain't never gonna allow any niggra
stoonts to go to Little Rock
Central High School on
my watch .... *Gov. Orville*
Faubus
We ain't ever gonna give up
segregation................ *Sen. Jesse Helms*
I can't remember if Li'l Abner and Daisy
Mae ever integrated Dogpatch.....*Al Capp*

T 007
I will call up the Arkansas National
Guard and order them to keep those
niggras outta our schools............*Faubus*
I will nationalize your National Guard
and order them to keep the peace
while those children go inside and
register ....*Eisenhower*
Y'alls come on down to mah whites-
only restaurant in Atlanna
and git yuhsels uh
free ax handle ....*Lester Maddox*

T 008
If we let them, Jim Crow could very
well return to the South.............*Elbie Jay*
If we'd listened to Strom Thurmond
back then, we wouldn't be
having all these race
problems now..................*Sen. Trent Lott*
You won't get that chance,
you're out of office
as of now ....*Pres. George*
W. Bush

T 009
Bully! And carry a big stick.................*TR*
Money changers!...............................*JC*
A chicken in every pot ....*HH*
The New Deal will prevail ....*FDR*
The buck stops here........................*HST*
I will go to Korea..............................*IKE*
Ich bin ein donut...............................*JFK*
Light is at the end of the tunnel ....*LBJ*
I have a dream ....*MLK*

T 010
The working class can kiss my ass,
I got the foreman's
job at last.......................*Manuel Labor*
Wall Street lays an egg.................*Variety*
I'm a jolly banker,
jolly banker am I.............*Woody Guthrie*

T 011
Brother, can you spare a dime?........*Bing*
Crosby
Prosperity is just around
the corner......................*Herbert Hoover*
Coal miners put down your picks
and shovels ....*John L. Lewis*
Truck drivers park your trucks........*Jimmy*
Hoffa
Auto workers unite...........*Walter Reuther*
Huelga, farm workers
unite ....*Cesar Chavez*

T 012
My Pinkerton goons will
break this strike.....................*Henry Ford*
If you've seen one redwood,
you've seen them all ....*Ronald Reagan*
Burn the tapes ....*Richard M. Nixon*
Human rights! ....*Jimmy Carter*

T 013
We are
not butchers!.............*George H.W. Bush*
There is no country today under
Communist control in eastern
Europe ....*Gerald Ford*
Jerry Ford can't fart and chew gum
at the same time ....*Lyndon*
B. Johnson
I studied dramatics under
MacArthur...........................*Eisenhower*

T 014
I did not schtup that woman.....*Slick Willy*
That child ain't mine ...*Warren G. Harding*
I admire Thomas Moore ....*Eugene*
McCarthy
I admire the Prince
of Peace ....*Ronald Reagan*
The president is a card-carrying
communist......*Tail Gunner Joe McCarthy*
I never said anything like that ....*Charlie*
McCarthy

T 015
I am not related to Charlie
McCarthy .... *Calija (Hank Williams)*
The daring young men in their flying
machines, they go uppity,
up, up, and down ditty down, down ... *Ron*
Goodwin

T 016
Martians have just landed
near Grover's Mill in
New Jersey .... *Orson Welles*
Emperor Ming must be
behind this .... *Flash Gordon*

T 017
The Hindenburg has caught
fire and is going down.... *Herbert Morrison*
I told them not to fill that thing
with hydrogen.............. *Charles Lindbergh*
How about some mock combat? .... *Waldo*
Pepper
Jawohl! .... *Ernst (Udet) Kessler*

T 018
Up, up, and away in my
beautiful balloon............................ *TWA*
Come fly with me......................... *Sinatra*
I'm leaving on a jet plane .... *Mary Travers*
Fly on Pan American
Airways............................... *Juan Trippe*

T 019
We needed all the scrap iron and oil
that was cut off........................ *Japanese*
General Staff
Americans are soft and lazy.............. *Tojo*
Banzai, banzai, banzai .... *Yamashita*
Why are the waves
so restless?................................ *Hirohito*
Tora Tora Tora........... *Lt. Cmdr. Fuchida*
This is a day that will
live in infamy..................................... *FDR*

T 020
I told them several times, but nobody
would believe me ...... *Lt. Cmdr. Rochefort*
I told them, but I was told
not to worry about it................. *Pvt. Elliott*
We've awakened a
sleeping giant .... *Yamamoto*
They will attack us
again at Midway................ *Joel Rochefort*

T 021
I'm sending back my Japanese medals
via air express to the emperor
himself............................ *Jimmy Doolittle*
I shall return............................ *MacArthur*
I'll be back .... *Schwarzenegger*
Four carriers and one battle cruiser
sunk at the Battle of Midway.......... *Nimitz*
Not a bad day's work................ *Spruance*
I shot down 27 enemy planes in the
Pacific, and then spent a year at the
Tokyo Hilton................. *Pappy Boyington*

T 022
No poor dumb bastard ever
won a war by dying for
his country..................... *George C. Scott*
The war starts here .... *Theodore*
Roosevelt Jr.
Our regiment liberated
Italy .... *Daniel Inouye*
Willy and Joe liberated
France................................. *Bill Mauldin*
Sad Sack stayed in Alabama....... *George*
Baker

T 023
Yea though I walk through the valley of
the Shadow of Death, I will fear no evil,
for I'm the meanest SOB in the
valley.......................... *George S. Patton*

T 024
You're surrounded und you must
surrender, now .... *General*
von Manteuffel
NUTS .... *General McAuliffe*
We are changing direction to
relieve General McAuliffe at
Bastogne .... *General Patton*

T 025
There's still lots of action flying for
Terry and the Pirates over the Hump
from Burma to and from eastern
China .... *Milton Caniff*
Beware Mount Suribachi .... *USMC*
Bomb them back
to the stone age .... *LeMay*

T 026
We made it,
and it works .... *General Groves*
Just me and my
Enola Gay .... *Paul Tibbets*
We can build a
bigger one .... *Edward Teller*
We must now endure
the unendurable .... *His Majesty*

T 027
Buy war bonds .... *Joe Louis*
Buy more war bonds .... *Clark Gable*
They're either too
young or too old .... *Rosemary Clooney*
'Til they come marching
home .... *Andrews Sisters*

U 001
The rising tide might lift
some of the boats .... *Jack Kennedy*
But if you don't have a boat, you're
gonna f___ing drown .... *Frank*
Fitzsimmons
We found the Titanic .... *Robert Ballard*
It was sad when the great ship
went down .... *Camp song*
Remember the great ore ship,
Edmund Fitzgerald .... *Gordon Lightfoot*

U 002
The Church must open up
and modernize .... *Pope John XXIII*
The Pill is a no-no .... *Pope Paul VI*
The first non-Italian pope in
500 years .... *Pope John Paul II*
I just couldn't take it any more .... *Pope*
Benedict XVI
Evolution and the Big
Bang are real .... *Pope Francisco*

U 003
We all live in a
Yellow Submarine .... *The Beatles*
They call me Mellow Yellow .... *Donovan*
The Great Yellow Bird .... *Sean Garrison*

U 004
Jambalaya, crawfish pie, and
filé gumbo, we'll have big fun on the
bayou .... *Hank Williams*
Come to the Big Easy
for Mardi Gras .... *Mayor Landrieu*
Laissez les bon
temps roller .... *King Creole*
Best Cajun chef in the
Vieux Carré .... *Paul Prudhomm*
Best Creole chef on Bourbon
Street .... *Emeril Lagasse*
Best soul food
in the Tremé ... *Aunt Jemima & Uncle Ben*
Best pig snouts and boiled
catfish on the levee .... *Porgy and Bass*

U 005
I drove my Chevy to the levee, but the
levee was dry, and them good ol' boys
was drinking whiskey and rye .... *Don*
McLean
There is a house in New Orleans that's
called the Rising Sun .... *The Animals*
Summertime, and the living is easy .... *Ella*
Fitzgerald
Sweet Georgia Brown .... *Ethel Waters*
Sweet Caroline .... *Neil Diamond*

U 006
Way down upon the
Chattahoochee................ *Stephen Foster*
Izzat the Chattanooga
Choo Choo?......................... *Glenn Miller*
I don't know...................... *Railroad porter*
Georgia out of my mind .... *Ray Charles*
Robinson
Roll me over in the clover .... *Sassy*
Lassies
I'm looking over a four-leaf
clover................................... *Art Mooney*

U 007
My pet cheetah loves walking with me
along the Champs Elysees in
Paris............................ *Josephine Baker*
Help me hold up this lampost...... *Marlene*
Dietrich
No thanks, I want
to be alone........................... *Greta Garbo*

U 008
You can learn a lot
from Lydia............................. *Geo. Burns*
Because we can........................ *Stepford*
husbands

U 009
Henry VIII married half a dozen
Queens, and I've married twenty-
one husbands .... *Zsa Gabor*
Don't get angry, get it all...... *Ivana Trump*

U 010
I'm taking Stevie Wonder
to lunch........................... *Wonder Woman*
I was the IT girl in the 1920s .... *Clara Bow*
I was one red hot mamma .... *Sophie*
Tucker
The way we weren't....... *Barbra Streisand*
I feel pretty, oh so pretty ..... *Natalie Wood*

U 011a
Let me entertain you...... *Gypsy Rose Lee*
They say I'm naughty .... *Bettie Paige*

U 011b
Come and see my twin 45s ... *Candy Barr*
Vote for Earl......................... *Blaze Starr*
Pornography? I can't define it,
but I knows it when I sees it........... *Potter*
Stewart

U 012
Some of my Samoan girls may have
misled me about their sex practices
in the western Pacific .... *Margaret Mead*
Sex is good, but largely
misunderstood .... *Alfred Kinsey*
Sex is good and now better-
understood .... *Masters & Johnson*
Sex is very good .... *Doctor Ruth*

U 013
All the world's
a stage .... *Wm. Shakespeare*
It's showtime......................... *Betelgeuse*
It's showtime, folks................ *Joe Gideon*
Come see my Wild
West Show .... *Buffalo Bill*
Come see the greatest
show on earth............... *Barnum & Bailey*

U 014
There's too many people
inside this tent........................ *J.A. Bailey*
Come and see the Egress.... *P.T. Barnum*
Come see two lion tamers get
eaten by lions .... *Siegfried & Roy*

U 015
Send in the clowns.............. *Emmett Kelly*
OK, here I am, all the others
can leave now................. *Bozo the Clown*
Send out the clowns, we
are now shutting down for
the last time .... *Ringling Brothers*
We will send all our
lions to a petting zoo .... *Roy & Siegfried*

U 016
Ah, yes, my little chickadee,
have you ever had
this tooth pulled before? ........*W.C. Fields*
Come up and see me sometime ....*Mae
West*

V 001
Come and see
my weiner .... *Anthony Weiner*
I can't get it up anymore .... *Willy Nilly*
Much ado about nothing .... *The Bard*
It's a small world after all ..*Sherman Bros.*
All hat and no cattle......... *Clint Murchison*

V 002
Beat it kid, you bother me .... *William C.
Fields*
I don't get no respect................... *Rodney
Dangerfield*
Here's Johnny! .... *Ed McMahon*
Here's Johnny! ....*Jack Nicholson*
I'm called Mr. Warmth.......... *Don Rickles*
No, you're called the Merchant
of Venom .... *Milton Berle*

V 003
How am I dooin? .... *Mayor Ed Koch*
Doo wop .... *The Cadillacs*
Do do that voodoo
that you do........................... *Cole Porter*
Do wacka do wacka do......... *Roger Miller*
Asparagus?
Ugh! Gumby doo doo .... *Joan Rivers*

V 004
I was born under a
wandering star ....*Lee Marvin*
And he was born to wander, the next-
of-kin to the wayward wind...... *Gogi Grant*

V 005
Cast your fate
to the winds .... *Vince Guaraldi*
I'm five hundred miles away from
home..................................... *Bobby Bare*
I hear the train a-coming, it's coming
round the bend.................... *Johnny Cash*

V 006
Politics ain't bean-bag ....*David Axelrod*
All politics are local .... *Tip O'Neill*
All politics are national.......*A. Abramowitz*
All we need is a good business
administration .... *George Babbitt*
All we need is a good
five-cent cigar .... *Thomas R.
Marshall*

V 007
Everyone loves Brighty, the Burro of
the Grand Canyon Bright Angel
Trail............................... *Margaret Henry*
Brighty is our
star attraction....................... *Park Ranger*
Seabiscuit was the world's
best horse ever.......... *Charles S. Howard*
No, Secretariat was........... *Chris & Penny
Chenery*

V 008
My horse is now a senator.......... *Caligula*
My kingdom for a horse........... *Richard III*
A horse is a horse of course..........*Mr. Ed*
Marezy doats
and doeszy doats.................*Milton Drake*
May the horse be
with you............................*Harrison Ford*
Best elementary
school in town...................... *Horse Mann*
My horse...
Ahh! A...Ahh! AAhh! .... *Jack Woltz*

V 009
What, me? Worry? ......*Alfred E. Newman*
I'm over 50 years old, and talkies are
coming soon, so should I be
worried?....................*Douglas Fairbanks*
Good night,
sweet prince...................*Charlie Chaplin*
What's selling?......................*J.C. Penny*
Was that Mr. Hoover at our
restaurant table? ....*Charlie Chaplin*
Mr. Chaplin is now banned from
re-entering the United States ......*J. Edgar
Hoover*

V 010
Did I really invent
baseball? ....*Abner Doubleday*
First in war, first in peace, and
last in the American
League ....*Washington Senators*
Except twice................*Walter "Big Train"
Johnson*
Anyone want to play
some cards? ....*Christie Mathewson*
Not in my clubhouse............*Connie Mack*
I made them change the rules in
seventy-seven....................*Ross Barnes*
Ball four, meat.....................*Crash Davis*
Fifty-nine wins in
eighty-four..............*Ole Hoss Radbourne*

V 011
Watch out Dutchman,
I'm coming down ....*Ty Cobb*
Watch your nose,
Cracker..........................*Honus Wagner*
Hit 'em where they ain't ....*Wee Willie
Keeler*
Four twenty-six in oh-one ....*Nap Lajoie*

V 012a
While playing in Mexico, when I
got hungry, I began to speak
pretty good Spanish ....*Josh Gibson*

V 012b
Don't look back, someone
might be gaining on you .....*Satchel Paige*
Life isn't a spectator sport.............*Jackie
Robinson*

V 013
Faster than a speeding
bullet ....*Cool Papa Bell*
Someone out in the center field
bleachers is shining a mirror in my
eyes .... *The Bambino*
I am the luckiest man on the
face of the earth....................*Lou Gehrig*

V014
There's a whole
lotta shakin' goin' on............*Elvis Presley*
The A's won the earthquake World
Series in California............. *Dave & Ricky
Henderson*
I was Gato Grande at
Mile High ....*Andrés Galarraga*
Sixty-one in sixty-one, and I hate
that damn asterisk................ *Roger Maris*

V 015
Four oh seven in forty-one.... *The Splinter*
Fifty-six straight in 41,
and how do I look?....................*Joltin' Joe*
Where have you gone,
Joe DiMaggio?........... *Simon & Garfunkel*
We finally beat the Yankees in the
World Series at Ebbets Field ....*Roy
Campanella*
I gave a lot of batters some friendly
chin music .... *Sal "The Barber" Maglie*

V 016a
Three ninety in 1980 ....*George Brett*
Three ninety-four in 1994 .....*Tony Gwynn*
I don't make history,
I catch fly balls ....*Willie Mays*

V 016b
Let's play another game .... *Ernie Banks*
What has ____ ____ and
catches flies? ....*Max Patkin*

V 017
Take me out to the
ball game...........................*Harry Caray*
One seventy-three in sixty-six........*Sandy
Koufax*
I hit 376 in forty-eight for the
Cardinals .... *Stan "The Man" Musial*
I hit a total of 369 homers for the
Pirates....................................*Ralph Kiner*
I hit 331 homers for the Tigers .... *Hank
Greenburg*

V 018
I had a better year than the Prez........*The
Babe*
Thirty wins in thirty-four ....*Dizzy Dean*

V 019
Good short stops gotta have good
hands ....*Phil "The Scooter" Rizzuto*
It ain't over 'til it's over............*Yogi Berra*
Whose on first?.....................*Lou Costello*
I don't know...........................*Bud Abbott*
No, I Don't Know's on third ...*Lou Costello*
I'm on first.............................*Hu jin tao*

V 020
The mighty Casey
has hit a homer ....*Ernest Thayer*
Believe it or not ....*Robert Ripley*

V 021
Nice guys finish last...............*Leo the Lip*
Play those minor leaguers?
Never!............................. *John McGraw*
So long, suckers...........*Arnold Rothstein*
It ain't so, kid......................*Shoeless Joe*
Yer all out ...... *Kenesaw Mountain Landis*

V 022
Come to my baseball saloon in
downtown Chicago.................*Harry Cary*
Come to my baseball saloon on Geary
Street in San Francisco........*Lefty O'Doul*
A Giants gift shop has been added
to Lefty's Pub...................*The Sous Chef*

V 023
Come see where our Fisherman's
Wharf Sea Food Grotto used to
be...*Dimaggio's*
Two pennants in Denver.......*Andy Cohen*
And that's where I learned how
to be a manager...................*Earl Weaver*

V 024
The more I practice, the
luckier I get...........................*Gary Player*
Golf is a contact sport ....*Tiger Woods*
Two or three goals in every match....*Pelé*
I was once a pretty good tennis
player....................................*Arthur Ashe*
Game, set, and match................*Venus &
Serena Williams*

V 025
Air Jordan......................*Michael Jordan*
Slam Dunk.......................*Magic Johnson*
I was just clowning
around.............................. *Goose Tatum*
Me too, and we made lots of
money doing it ....*Meadowlark Lemon*
Everyone roots for David, but not
Goliath..........................*Wilt Chamberlain*
Love them Lakers ....*George Mikan*
Love them Phillips 66ers ....*Vernon
Vaughn*

V 026a
I am the greatest.............*Mohammed Ali*
Sugar Ray and me beat each
other up several times......*Jake Lammata*

V 026b
I can lick anyone in the bar .... *John L. Sullivan*
He knocked me out of the ring .... *Jack Dempsey*
I went 15 rounds with the dancing bear .... *Jimmy Braddock*
They can run, but they can't hide .... *The Brown Bomber*
What doesn't kill me makes me stronger .... *Frederich Nietzche*

V 027
I like to read comic books. They have better outcomes than in real life .... *Joe Palooka*
Somebody down there hates me .... *Rocky Grazziano*
I caught him with my toonderbolt .... *Ingemar Johansson*
He bit my ear off .... *Evander Holyfield*
I beat them all .... *Rocky Marciano*

V 028
Jumping Jack Flash is a gas gas gas .... *Rolling Stones*
I don't get no satisfaction ...... *Mick Jagger*
You're so vain .... *Carly Simon*

V 029
The Book of Mormon is chloroform in print and the world's best antidote for insomnia .... *Mark Twain*
Boredom is the awareness of time passing .... *Heidegger*
Never be bored .... *The Boz*
Come to the Cabaret where no one is ever bored .... *Joel Grey*

W 001
Hit the road, Jack, and don't you come back no more .... *The Raylettes*
What'd you say? .... *Ray Charles*
Road trip! .... *Otter & Boone*
Let's roll .... *Thelma & Louise*
And away we go .... *Jackie Gleason*

W 002
This ain't the place .... *Brigham Young*
Everyone in Utah is Mormon, even if they aren't Mormon .... *Jim McMahon*
Oh, when the Saints go marching out .... *Louis Armstrong*
We're off to see the Lizard .... *Dorothy*
Follow the yellow brick road .... *Head Munchkin*

W 003
When you come to the fork in the road, take it .... *Lawrence P. "Yogi" Berra*
Tip-toe through the tulips .... *Tiny Tim*
Happy trails to you .... *Roy Rogers*
Back in the saddle again .... *Gene Autry*
On the road .... *Jack Kerouac*
On the commode again .... *Willie Nelson*

W 004
Come see my act at the Purple Onion in San Francisco .... *Lenny Bruce*
Come and read some of the books in my basement bookstore ..... *Ferlinghetti*
I saw the best minds of my generation destroyed by madness and starvation .... *Allan Ginsberg*
I saw the best root vegetables of my generation plucked from the soil by evil machinery .... *The Beet Poet*

W 005
Break on through to the other side .... *Jim Morrison*
Where have all the flowers gone? .... *Peter, Mary, & Paul*
Under the Boardwalk .... *The Drifters*
This is the Dawning of the Age of Aquarius .... *The Fifth Dimension*
Tune in, turn on, drop dead .... *Timothy Leary*
Like a Virgin .... *Madonna*
Like a Sturgeon .... *Weird Al Yankovic*

W 006
Grass is good...............Nebuchadnezzar
Grass is very good .... *Cheech & Chong*
Ganja is good for you ....*Haile Selassie*
Rastafari
Guinness is good for you ....*Edward*
Guinness

W 007
Jah lives cause ganja .... *Bob Marley*
Rocky Mountain high............ *Bob Denver*
Puff the
Magic Dragon............*Peter, Paul, & Mary*
The High and the Mighty..............*Dimitry*
Tiomkin

W 008
A jelly donut? IN YOUR FOOT
LOCKER?!....................*Sgt. R. Lee Ermy*
Get your fat ass off my
obstacle! .... *Gunny Sgt. Hartman*
Good Morning
Viet Nam!....................*Adrian Cronhauer*
Follow the Ho Chi Minh trail............*Robin*
Williams
Hoo dat don dar? .... *Cao Dai*
Stop calling me a conniving
military con-artist.............. *Sergeant Bilko*

W 009
I'm not trying to seduce you,
Benjamin........................ *Mrs. Robinson*
God bless you please, Mrs.
Robinson ....*Simon & Garfunkel*

W 010
What's the worst fraternity on campus?
The one that sent a cadaver to the
faculty luncheon .... *Dean Wormer*
Do you still want to show me your
cucumber?.......................*Mrs. Wormer*
Mrs. Wormer will be vacationing in
Sarasota .... *Daily Faberian*

W 011
Louie, Louie.....................*The Kingsmen*
Toga, Toga, Toga ....*Bluto Blutarski*
A little bit softer now, a little
bit louder now .... *Otis Day &*
The Knights
Schtup her, you know
she wants it .... *The Devil (Geo. Carlin)*
There will be no more loud-speakers,
bullhorns, sit-ins, hoe-downs, or
shivarees on my campus....................*S.I.*
Hayakowa

W 012
The state budget has been looted
by the Democrats............ *Ronald Reagan*
Hey, c'mon Ron, what's the matter with
you? The election's over......... *Jeth Unruh*
Extremism is no vice, and I am not
insane .... *Barry Goldwater*

W 013
Who's the greatest pilot
you ever saw? .... *Gordo Cooper*
Anyone going up in that thing is going
to be just spam in a can .... *Chuck*
Yeager
That's one small step for a man, one
giant leap for mankind...... *Neil Armstrong*
Some people are saying the landings
on the Moon never happened.... *YouTube*

W 014
First American in outer space.......... *John*
Glenn
Sorry guys, I couldn't make it........... *Gus*
Grissom
Our Germans are better than their
Germans .... *Wherner von Braun*

X 001
East side, west side, all around the
town, boys and girls together on the
sidewalks of New York............*Charles B.*
Lawler
New York, New York. If I make it here,
I can make it anywhere ......*Kander & Ebb*

X 002
On Broadway ....George Benson
I love New York......... Fiorello LaGuardia
There's no people like
show people.................... Ethel Merman

X 003
The sounds of silence are written on
the subway walls .... Simon & Garfunkel
When you wish upon a star, it doesn't
matter who you are.............. Walt Disney
I'd like to teach the world to sing in
perfect harmony .... Billy Davis &
                                 Don Draper
If not, then the
Candyman can................. Sammy Davis

X 004
We started out as
the Quarrymen.................... The Beatles
Like a Limestone Cowboy............. Glenn
                                 Campbell
Like that'll be the day........... Buddy Holly

X 005
Oh, what a beautiful
morning .... Gordon McRae
It's a beautiful day in the
neighborhood........................Mr. Rogers
What a wonderful day................ Satchmo
This land is my land
and your land.......................Pete Seeger
See the USA in your one-horse
shay...................................... Doris Day

X 006a
Hundreds of thousands .... Ray Kroc
Millions and millions ....John D.
                                 Rockefeller
Billions and billions .... Carl Sagan

X 006b
Trillions and trillions...........Warren Buffett
Parsecs and
parsecs.....................Starship Enterprise
Googolplexes and googolplexes..........Ed
                                 Kasner

X 007
Shazam............................. Capt. Marvel
Arrrrrr .... Long John Silver
Fee, fi, fo, fum.....................Hungry Giant
Ho, ho, ho........................... Green Giant
Roar grrrrr snort..........Leo the MGM Lion
Hi dee hi dee hi dee ho ......Cab Calloway
Tutti-frutti, alla-rootie ....Little Richard

X 008
Aaa-ah-ah-aaa!........................... Tarzan
Great balls of fire.............Jerry Lee Lewis
Para bailar la Bamba.........Ritchie Valens
Peace, love, dope .... Terence Mann

X 009
Oh, there's rioting in Africa and there's
strife in Iran. The French hate the
Dutch and the Dutch hate Sudan.
And we don't like anybody
very much.................... The Kingston Trio
Daylight come and me wan go
home.............................. Harry Belafonte

X 010
Didn't need no welfare state.
Everybody pulled his weight. Those
were the days ....Archie &
                                 Edith Bunker

X 011
Dick Nixon has left a trail of s__t
behind him so deep it can fertilize
the entire Sinai........ Gen. Taylor in 'Good
                                 Morning, Vietnam'

X 012
Why was there a Watergate
break-in?..............*Bernstein & Woodward*
Who was Deep Throat?.......... *Woodward
& Bernstein*
I was Deep Throat........... *Linda Lovelace*
Follow the money.................*Deep Throat*

X 013
We're going to put Watergate behind
us and get along with the business of
of America ....*Richard Millhous Nixon*

X 014
This is my last news conference and
you news reporters won't have Nixon
to kick around anymore .... *Millhous*
I was Deep Throat.............. *W. Mark Felt*

Y 001
Only little people pay taxes............ *Leona
Helmsley*
You, madam, are a feculent
wretch...........................*Truman Capote*
I don't pay taxes either, and
I've pawed many women
in my time ....*Donald Trumpski*
I hate rich people who avoid
paying taxes................. *James Michener*

Y 002
Everybody loves somebody
sometimes ....*Dino Martin*
Everybody loves me................. *Trumpski*
Trust me, what do you have to
lose?...*Trump*
Bad, Bad, Leroy Trump,
baddest man in the whole
damn dump...........................*Jim Croce*
Trump is a fake, a fraud, a crook,
and a liar.....................*Keith Olbermann*
Too bad Trump isn't Catholic, he
could be excommunicated ....*Megyn Kelly*

Y 003
Trump should step down.................*Pope
Francisco*
Trumpski is an idiot........ *Rosie O'Donnell*
Trump is a f___ing moron..........*Sec. Rex
Tillerson*
Shouldn't Trump (née Drumpf)
have gone to president
school?.......................... *Anna Kasperion*

Y 004
Let's have a big military parade in
Washington, just like the ones in North
Korea .... *Trump*
Yeah, like a military parade every
once in a while is a healthy thing ......*Rich
Lowry*

Y 005
Trump is the nation's biggest liar and
con-artist .... *George F. Will*
Yeah, even Ray Charles
can see that..........................*Cenk Uygur*
So can Mr. Magoo....................*Mel Blanc*

Y 006
Come and see what supply-side
finance and trickle-down economics
has done to Kansas ....*Gov. Sam
Brownback*
Don't bother........ *Kansas Supreme Court*

Y 007
Could I have won
that election? ....*Joe Biden*
Don't ask..................................... *Hillary*
Only the Shadow knows.............. *Lamont
Cranston*
Maybe I know .... *Mandrake the Magician*
Or maybe I do.......................... *Uri Geller*

Y 008

It's good to be king .... *Mel Brooks*
Every man a king .... *Huey Long*
I can't forget I was
once a king .... *Edward VIII*
I was king for a little while .... *King Ralph*
I hate those +#!*^! little
airplanes .... *King Kong*
Holy macaroon, Andy .... *The Kingfish*

Y 009

Everything I know is in the
newspapers .... *Will Rogers*
Don't believe everything you
read in the papers .... *Snopes.com*
Everything is
Fake News .... *Donald Trump*
Don't believe everything
you see online or on TV .... *David Mikkelson*
I deconstruct wide spread
rumors, urban legends,
and hoaxes .... *David Emery*

Y 010

You're now in The Twilight Zone .... *Rod Serling*
Go where no man has gone
before .... *William Shatner*
Live long and prosper ...... *Leonard Nimoy*
Beam me up Scotty .... *Capt. Kirk*
Stop the bubble
machine .... *Lawrence Welk*

Y 011

Bon appétit .... *Julia Child*
Not too hot, not too cold .... *Goldilocks*
What's for dinner? .... *Alfie Packer*
Spotted owl .... *Paul Bunyan*
Life is like a river .... *Atticus Finch*

Y 012

Life is but a dream .... *Rip Van Winkle*
Come and see
my vintage cars .... *Jay Leno*
The man who dies rich dies
disgraced .... *Andrew Carnegie*
I seldom attend my own garden
parties .... *Jay Gatsby*

Y 013

Can't buy me love .... *John, Paul, Ringo, & George*
I'm proof you can't buy happiness
and friendship .... *Doris Duke*
This poor little rich girl has
nothing left .... *Barbara Hutton*

Y 014

The coldest winter I ever spent was a
summer in San Francisco ...... *Mark Twain*
I left my heart in
San Francisco .... *Tony Bennett*
Open up your Golden Gate.
San Francisco, here I come ...... *Jeannette McDonald*
All the Hippies who came to San
Francisco for the Summer of Love
froze their little tushies off in Golden
Gate Park .... *Mayor Alioto*

Z 001

Come to our Edinburgh Castle Scottish
Pub on Geary Street .... *Clan Francisco*
Is my edict good
for a beer? .... *Emperor Norton*

Z 002

Come visit my City Lights Bookstore in
North Beach .... *Larry Ferlinghetti*
Don't call it Frisco .... *Herb Caen*
I am the King of Torts .... *Melvin Belli*
I stole them torts and took them
clean away .... *The Knave of Harps*

Z 003
That's life, and it was a very good year,
and I did it my way.............. *Frank Sinatra*
All is news reporting ....*Lowell Thomas*
No gnus is good gnus..................*Aesop*
It's time to take
a closer look...................... *Seth Meyers*

Z 004
Life is nasty, brutish,
and short...................... *Thomas Hobbes*
Life is a dead-end street .... *H.L. Mencken*
Life's a bitch, then you die ....*Anthony
Cruz*
Life's a bowl of cherries ....*Zachary Taylor*
Have another cherry?.....*Daryl van Horne*
Life is like a box
of chocolates..................... *Forrest Gump*

Z 005
Ah, make the most of what we yet may
spend, before we too unto the dust
descend. Dust unto dust and
under dust to lie; no wine,
no rhyme, no end ....*Kalil Gibran*
In the end, we are all dead......*J. Maynard
Keynes*

Z 006
When it's time, Santa Muerte comes
and gently takes away
suffering.................... *Mexican folk belief*
Dead men tell no tales............*Capt. Kidd*
The past is never dead...... *Wm. Faulkner*
There are no second acts ....*F. Scott
Fitzgerald*

Z 007
Oh? Izzat so?............................ *Lazarus*
What kind of
second acts?.................... *Bridey Murphy*
You mean like in India? .... *Nehru*
I'm never gonna die.............. *Don Rickles*

Z 008
As time goes by .... *Sam, on the piano*
We Germans have to operate in all
different kinds of conditions .... *Major
Strasser*
There are some neighborhoods in New
York I wouldn't advise you
to invade......................................*Bogart*
Major Strasser has been shot. Round
up the usual suspects .... *Capt. Renault*
Louie, I think this is the beginning
of a beautiful friendship ....*Rick Blaine*

Z 009
All good things must come to an
end..*Chaucer*
" ____________ " .... *Marcel Marceau*

Z 010
Frankly my dear, I don't
give a damn..........................*Rhett Butler*
Thanks for the memories..........*Bob Hope*
Rosebud......................*John Foster Kane*
Checkmate ....*Bobby Fischer*
Hi-yo Silver, away .... *Lone Ranger*
You betchum, Red Ryder .....*Little Beaver*
Gitemup, Scout.............................. *Tonto*

Z 011
Now I am become death, destroyer of
worlds (from the Bhagavad
Gita)................................. *Oppenheimer*
She's-a go Boom .... *Enrico Fermi*
We can build a
bigger one ....*Edward Teller*

Z 012
This is London, and we are still
here. Good night.........*Edward R. Murrow*
And that's the way it wasn't ....*Walter
Cronkite*
Say good night, David ....*Chet Huntley*
Good night, David ....*David Brinkley*

Z 013
At the end of time, we'll play the March
of the Marionettes .... *Alfred Hitchcock*
At the end of time, good will triumph
over evil .... *The Zoroastrian Gathas*
At the end of time, I will blow my conch
shell to announce the coming of the
great and terrible
Judgment Day...... *The Archangel Gabriel*
How about the great
and terrible Oz? .... *The Wizard*
At the end of time, I'll stop short,
never to go again .... *Grandfather Clock*
At the end of time, time itself
will cease to exist .... *Father Time*

Z 014
At the end of time, Satan will be
defeated .... *The Archangel Michael*
At the end of time, Lord Shiva and Kali
will come and destroy everything in the
material universe........... *The Vache Veda*

Z 015
At the end of time, the last person on
Earth will expire, and existence will be
transformed once again into
bupkis....................................... *YHWH*

Z 016
After the end of time, Lord Brahma
will start everything up again........ *The Big
Veda*
Good and evil will once again
contend.................... *The Magian Gathas*
And the sea shall
give up her dead .... *Book of Common
Prayer, 1789*

Z 017
After the end of time, the New Year's
Baby will come back into existence at
midnight on New Year's Day, and time
will start all over again .... *Father Time*

Z 018
After the end of time, there will be a
new beginning and a new Adam and
Eve........................ *Nathaniel Hawthorne*
Would you like a
magic mushroom? .... *Eve*
Yeah, why not? .... *Adam*
Hey, who asked you?.... *The Fallen Angel*
Hi ho, hi ho, it's back to
work we go .... *The Seven Dwarves*

Z 019
That is all......... *M*A*S*H* P-A announcer*

BEGINNING DATES of SELECTED ANCIENT WORLD CITIES, MONUMENTS, and CALENDARS

Gobekli Tepe (built) .... ca. 9000 BC
Catal Huyuk (settled) .... 7500 BC
Ninevah (settled) .... ca. 6000 BC
Ashkelon (settled) .... 5900 BC
1st Sothic Cycle (backdated) ..... 5683 BC
Greek Torah (Septuagian)* .... 5554 BC
Byzantine (Alexandria)* .... 5492 BC
Hebrew Torah
(Fla. Josephus)* .... 5467 BC
Sumerian King List* .... ca. 4500 BC
Great Sphinx of Giza .... ca. 4500 BC
2nd Sothic Cycle (backdated) ..... 4241 BC
Hebrew Torah (Masoretic)* .... 4174 BC
Archbishop of Usher* .... 4004 BC
Hebrew Calendar*
(backdated) .... 3761 BC
Anno Mundi (Bede)* .... 2952 BC
Chinese (Fu-xi)* .... 2852 BC
City of Ur (founded) .... 2800 BC
3rd Sothic Cycle (1460 years) .... 2763 BC
Jewish (biblical)* .... 2761 BC
Anno Mundi (Septuagint)* .... 2750 BC
Coptic* .... 2670 BC
Chinese (Huang di)* .... 2627 BC
Mohenjodaro (occupied) .... ca. 2600 BC
Byblos (founded) .... ca. 2600 BC
Great Pyramid of Giza .... 2580 BC
City of Lagash (founded) .... 2500 BC
Armenian* .... 2492 BC
Stonehenge (built) .... ca. 2400 BC
Akkadian (Sargon I)* .... 2224 BC
Babylon (founded) .... 2200 BC
City of Eridu (founded) .... ca. 2200 BC
Carnac stones (built) .... ca. 2200 BC
Mayan Long Count* .... 2114 BC
Hindu (Kali Yuga)* .... 2102 BC
Egyptian (1st dynasty)* .... 2100 BC
Xia Dynasty (China)* .... 2070 BC
Neo Sumerian (Umma)* .... 2000 BC
Troy (founded) .... ca. 2000 BC
Knossis (settled) .... ca. 2000 BC
Laguna Pueblo (settled) .... ca. 2000 BC

Jerusalem (founded) .... 2000 BC
Newgrange (built) .... ca. 2000 BC
Babylonian (Hammurabi)* .... 1792 BC
Shang Dynasty (China)* .... 1600 BC
Delphic Oracle (origin) .... ca. 1400 BC
Olmec settlements .... ca. 1200 BC
Zhou Dynasty (China)* .... 1046 BC
Carthage (founded)* .... 846 BC
First Olympiad* .... 776 BC
Rome AUC (founded)* .... 752 BC
Babylonian (Nabonassar)* .... 747 BC
Japanese (Jimmu)* .... 660 BC
Byzantium (settled) .... 657 BC
Zoroastrian (Achaemenid)* .... 650 BC
Buddhist (Siamese)* .... 542 BC
Monte Alba (Mexico) .... ca. 500 BC
Halley's Comet (China) .... 467 BC
Han Dynasty (China)* .... 206 BC
Teotihuacon (built) .... 150 BC
Tang Dynasty* .... 618 CE
Islamic (Hegeira)* .... 622 CE
Vinland (settlement) .... ca. 1000 CE
Mixtec Codices .... 1050 CE
Zimbabwe (built) .... ca. 1050 CE
Battle Abbey (opened) .... 1067 CE
Angkor Watt (built) .... 1112 CE
Cahokia Mounds (built) .... ca. 1200 CE
Tenochtitlan (settled) .... 1225 CE
Santo Domingo .... 1496 CE
San Juan, PR (founded) .... 1509 CE
Havana (settled) .... 1515 CE
Mexico City (taken) .... 1518 CE
Fort Caroline (settled) .... 1564 CE
St. Augustine (settled) .... 1565 CE
Roanoke Colony .... 1585 CE
Jamestown Colony .... 1607 CE
Quebec .... 1608 CE

Refers to a calendar

ABOUT THE AUTHOR

Hal Elliott is an emeritus professor of geography from Weber State University in Ogden, Utah. He graduated from San Francisco State University with a BA degree in History & Philosophy and an MA degree in Geography. He later studied Chinese (Mandarin) from the University of California Extension, and graduated from the University of Oklahoma with a PhD in Geography & Asian Studies. He has taught classes in World Geography, Geography of the U.S. & Canada, Europe, Middle East, Asia, China, and India. He also has taught classes on the History of Early Western Civilization and the History of Early Eastern Civilization. He has published articles in *The Journal of Geography, Geographical Analysis, The Southeastern Geographer, Economic Geography, Urban Geography, Ecumene, The Yearbook of the Association of Pacific Coast Geographers,*  *The Florida Geographer, The Professional Geographer, The California Geographer, The Annals of Regional Science, The Scottish American Patriot*, and *The Ohio Genealogical Quarterly.* Before his position at WSU, he taught classes at the College of San Mateo (CA), Cameron State College (OK), and Florida International University.

Thanks to Dr. Sarah A. Elliott, who helped considerably in bringing this manuscript into print.

No animals were harmed in the making of this book. : -)

Cheers......................HME, March 2018